ALSO BY THE ANDERSONS

Changing the Dream - A Pilgrimage to Machu Picchu
Walking the Beauty Way - Musical CD

—The—
Beauty Way

Ceremonial Shamanism

LAURA AND MICHAEL ANDERSON

BALBOA.
PRESS

A DIVISION OF HAY HOUSE

Balboa Press books may be ordered through booksellers or by contacting:

Balboa Press
A Division of Hay House
1663 Liberty Drive
Bloomington, IN 47403
www.balboapress.com
1 (877) 407-4847

Printed in the United States of America.

ISBN: 978-1-4525-2257-9 (sc)
ISBN: 978-1-4525-2256-2 (hc)
ISBN: 978-1-4525-2258-6 (e)

Library of Congress Control Number: 2014916972

Balboa Press rev. date: 2/9/2015

This work is dedicated to the Spirit of *Pachakuti*
who made it our purpose to share the
teaching of *The Beauty Way.*

To my husband Michael, who encouraged, supported,
and assisted me every step of the way. And to our
children and grandchildren, you are our legacy.

To my friends, especially Cassie Measures who supported and
assisted me with editing and aspects of comprehension, and
Dee Prigmore, *Neutrina Spirit Walker* whose contemplation and
discussion with me on the elements has been invaluable.

INTRODUCTION

Shamanism as a spiritual practice does not require any specific religious beliefs, but rather encourages practitioners to discover animalism, an ancient world view of our ancestors. This belief is that all created things: human, animal, plant, landscapes, elements, and seasons have an intelligent, communicative life force or spirit. As children, most of us have had spontaneous Shamanic experiences, accompanied by a strong sense of oneness with the Universe. These are what we call mystical experiences. Most children have an inner knowing that energy, or life force resides in all things. They start out as potential Shaman.

At the heart of all Shamanism are also controlled visionary experiences that connects the practitioner with spirit beings who guide, guard, instruct, and bless life. These spirit beings include Power Animals, or Spirit Guides.

Actually, all energy techniques are Shamanic in nature. Reiki, Feng Shui, Yoga, T'ai Chi/Chi Kung and many forms of Divination are based on the belief in a life force energy that can be worked with and channeled. Yet the difference in just working with energy and being a Shamanic Practitioner is in the action taken. A Shaman actively shifts, transmutes, removes and recovers energy for themselves or a client. They mediate for their 'tribe'. They actively work to shift the dream of society through ceremony and meditation for the betterment of humanity. Anyone with an interest in and dedication to Shamanic wisdom can become a Shamanic practitioner, someone who searches through the darkness of life for a personal spiritual path that that is creative, life affirming and joyful.

Michael and I have been doing Ceremony in various forms and styles since the early 1990's. Our personal spiritual quests have led us to understand that it is through Ceremony we connect to the Divine, not abstract knowledge. That is why the Beauty Way is called Ceremonial Shamanism. Our action toward connecting to the Divine, and shifting energy is done through ceremony. We love teaching, lecturing and talking about various spiritual truths but now have internalized the knowing that it is through ceremony humanity connects to the Source within, and that has made all the difference.

This book was compiled from our lectures, notes, and the information we share during the Peruvian Shaman classes we began teaching after we returned from our pilgrimage to Peru in 2011. With each series of classes we taught, we would add, reorganize, or let go of information in an attempt to make the ideas easier and quicker to grasp. I soon realized that the revelations we received from this information are for every healer or seeker, not just those that are taking energetic connective ceremonies or Shamanic Rites. Most of the book revolves around information I use with the various energetic ceremonies of the Munay-Ki in order to help my students get a deeper understanding of that modality. However, I believe the information presented will be life changing in its own right, with or without the energetic ceremonies. For those that practice Shamanism, the exercises and information make it easier to stay connected to the Beauty Way.

(5-17-11)
(From my journal – Laura Anderson)

I had to push away the daily thoughts during the ceremony reminding myself that this was sacred and important. I felt the enveloping of Michael's energy as he began the ceremony of the first Rite. Then during the ceremony I saw Machu Picchu in Peru, growing larger and larger, and I was looking out towards it. I reminded myself the journey is about me now, and when Michael blew into my hands to activate the healer, I felt the wind at Machu Picchu surrounding me. I remembered that the crow is with me and I am a shape shifter now. During the journey I was in the lap of Pachamama, the great Mother at Machu Picchu, Peru. I was the observer and the observed. My journey, or walk was to the tree in the center courtyard and I had to fight the mind a couple of times to let go of the day and stay there. While there, I saw the healers of the ancient world, the sacred tree of life, yet I continued to be both the observer and the observed. It was unique to me to be both simultaneously. I knew then, this would be life changing.

Contents

CHAPTER 1

The Beauty Way

We are many nodes in a sacred space, forwarded from the
Ancestors, into the Golden Age of Dreaming.
- Michael Anderson

The Beauty Way is a way of approaching life that empowers and uplifts us by giving us the chance to choose our reality instead of continuing to live with what we have created from a place of disempowerment. It is a practice where we notice, then comment on those things that are beautiful around us, and in doing so create a life of beauty. We create a life of peace and prosperity by first seeing them, then embodying them.

All things are possible and present before us, both those things that cause disharmony as well as those things that are lovely. Both the rose and the thorn are on the bush. Which do we notice first? And which do we comment on and point out to others? Our free will or choice is our greatest gift, and our choice creates our experiences. So many people in our world are trapped in the disempowering story of the human race consciousness, programmed to live a life of disempowerment due to that programming. The Beauty Way teaches us how to break free of that programming. It gives us the understanding and tools to live a life of Beauty. This is the Beauty Way, a way of choice and self-empowerment.

Let us begin by stating that Shamanism is the oldest form of Spirituality known to man. A Shaman is a man or woman of power who calls on the forces of nature for assistance in gaining information and healing for both physical and emotional wounds. They act as intermediaries between the physical and non–physical world to help both themselves and others regain lost power and remove excessive or intrusive energy. Their work includes assistance through soul retrieval, energy extractions or energy clearing. They take action for their clients and the world at large.

The Shaman's path is the way of light and energy. They work to overcome their own self-limiting ideas and to be free of the opinions of others so that they can assist themselves and others without judgment. The Beauty Way teaches the Shaman is to be alert at all times to synchronicity, to listen to messages from nature, and strive to create harmony between their thoughts, things, and events. Acknowledging the wholeness of being that is the Earth, they learn to sense the interconnectedness of the visible and invisible Universe.

A Shaman recognizes that everything is alive and that objects have the ability to retain information that can be accessed to help them with their goals. They work with energy. A true Shaman will tailor their techniques to individual needs. They work with and know many healing modalities and are open to using the one that works best at the specific time. The main way they access the spirit world for information or assistance is through journey. It is similar to a guided meditation. In the past they were chosen to be Shaman. The elders of their tribe would choose them, and at the appropriate time put them through difficult initiations. Often, they were considered chosen by the Universe after experiencing a traumatic event like being struck by lightning or having a near death experience. Some would be born cross eyed, or with a physical disability that were considered signs of Shamanic ability. In today's world, with education and through Ceremonial Initiation or Rites, people can choose to become a Shaman and work with energy.

It seems that most people on a spiritual path find themselves in a constant struggle believing that the struggle is the spiritual path, but it is not. Through Ceremonial Shamanic initiations we gain powerful assistance by connecting to a lineage of Earth Keepers, healers and energy workers that came before us, or will come after us. Through this connection these Earth Keepers will begin to assist us in our personal healing making our spiritual path one of ease, one of beauty.

There are many valid Shamanic traditions. I consider Reiki a Shamanic modality as it also connects us to a lineage. However, this book focuses mostly on the Beauty Way, Ceremonial Peruvian Shamanism. It is based on what we learned through the Munay-Ki Rites, the Andean Mountain Shamanic initiations or energy connections. It was the style we had studied prior to and began teaching when we returned from Machu Picchu, Peru. The most powerful lesson I learned from this modality was that most of our personal struggle comes from our own personal wounds. That we must learn how to clear them if we want to live the Beauty Way. Healing others is a very noble profession, but until we heal ourselves, our dream, our reality, will not change. It is from a healed place that we are able to manifest our dreams and desires, that we are better able to assist others on their healing journey.

> *"The Munay - Ki Rites are the Initiation Rites of the Medicine people of the Americas. They are a nine step process for healing the wounds of our past childhood and the wounds of our ancestors; both the genetic and karmic inheritance that we were born into this life with. It is a fast track to enlightenment. Receiving the Munay-Ki Rites will also clear the energy centers, allowing you to begin to acquire a luminous rainbow body. The later initiations alter your DNA and allow you to create a new body that heals or ages differently, becoming a Homo Luminous being.*
>
> Paraphrased from "Healing the Luminous Body" - Alberto Villoldo, Ph.D.

When performing the Munay-Ki Rites, many teachers use a Pi stone, a round stone with a hole in the center that represents the Luminous Energy Field around each of us. This Energy Field surrounds and informs us. It is a blueprint for our physical, emotional and spiritual self. Many modalities call it the aura. When we change, reprogram and clear this energy field, we change our world, our personal dream. The Pi stone also represents the hyper dimensional gateway that gives a Shaman access to the invisible realms during journey. Various modalities use different ways to ceremonially connect a student to the lineage of their tradition when energetically connecting them to a specific lineage. The Shaman of the Muany-Ki use a Pi stone.

Pi stones can be found in museums, antique shops, trade days, and many other places all around the Americas. Few Archeologists know what they were used for, but Peruvian Shamanism teaches they are representations of an access point to the matrix of creation. After completing the Munay-Ki Rites the Shaman becomes this portal represented by the stone. The stone then becomes a reminder that they are always, as Shaman, able to access this matrix of creation. This access allows them to dream the world into being by choice, to change their current dream, no longer having to settle for a life that is the effect of their past programing. They are able to create a life or dream from choice as a result of future possibilities. This makes their destiny always available to them.

The Pi stone can also become an object of power for them. If given by a teacher, this stone also connects the owner to the place where the teacher received Shamanic Rites of passage, or became a medicine person. It will connect them to their teacher's power to assist them as well. Any object of power gifted to a Shamanic Practitioner, to anyone for that matter, holds a connection to the presenter's power.

In the Andean tradition, the Pi stone becomes an organizing principle in the Shaman's mesa or traveling altar and begins to organize their relationship to knowledge or power. It becomes a key stone or the center of a personal mesa, or traveling altar.

During the Ceremonial Energetic Connection, or nine Rites of the Munay-Ki, seeds of possibility are placed in the student's personal Energy Field. They then become responsible for growing them, "into corn, or fruit bearing trees". This is where, in my mind, the information in the following chapters has so much value. The information or knowledge helps their understanding or seeds to grow. It helps clear energetic wounds so these 'seeds of possibility' can be used to the student's advantage resulting in a change of their personal reality.

The Andean Culture is one of agriculture, so the concept of planting seeds is the image presented with this Shamanic Rite modality. This form has Nine Rites. Four Rites or Ceremonies they consider fundamental or foundational rights. Four lineage Rites or Ceremonies that connect to a lineage of past and future luminous beings. The last Rite or Ceremony allows the receiver to become an access point to the matrix of creation, giving them the ability to create their own dream. In our class series, we include a manifestation ceremony from South America called the Despacho, a ceremony of appreciation. Since we know it is through gratitude that we manifest, it seems appropriate to include how to do this ceremony in our class series.

A short explanation or definition of the Initiation Rites of the Munay-Ki are in the appendix chapter which may be helpful if you are interested in them. However, the information in this book will serve any seeker on the spiritual path, with or without taking the Munay-ki Rites.

What we love so much about the Andean Wisdom is it feels timeless. Although it comes from the same universal source of truth as all esoteric teachings, it is unique in that it forms a continuous cultural thread from before the Inka to the present time. When the Spanish came to Peru, the Shaman went into the mountains to protect their Rites or processes and prophecies. The teachings and Munay-Ki Rites come as a direct line, unadulterated. Their Rites are a very pure and simple connection to truth. It is not a religion or philosophy but a way of life that embodies ethical, moral, and spiritual guidelines. The purpose of human life to the Andean Shaman, as we understand it, is to achieve and maintain balance between the human sphere and the natural world, to live harmoniously. In this way you achieve inner peace. When you have inner peace, you are happy and healthy. The healing message as we understand it is simple but powerful. It teaches to be healed and happy we must clear the heart, love deeply, harmonize our thoughts and feelings, align our efforts to do our best and respect the natural environment.

A summary of the story of the Peruvian Shaman that we are studying is they went into the mountains to escape persecution and preserve their traditions when the Spanish came to conquer the Inka. Secluded in the high mountains they were able to keep their life style and body of processes, or ceremonies pure. They came down from the mountains in 2006 to share their Munay-Ki Rites with the planet. They believe the North and South are to come together to usher in the new age of peace, and they felt that this was the time to help and encourage that coming together by sharing their teachings and Shamanic Rites. They encourage Shamanic practitioners and healers in the North to learn and take the Munay-Ki Shamanic Rites, to connect to the Earth Keepers and the processes of the South. I would encourage anyone interested to find a teacher for the connections ceremonies, but in truth, you will make a shift from the information to come. If you are a teacher of the Munay-Ki I would invite you to use the information to accompany your class as we have found it to be a powerful assistance in the student's shift.

Similar to most spiritual traditions, there are ethical principles in the teachings of the Munay-Ki that we have adopted for the Beauty Way course. These principles demonstrate the earth based world view of the Q'ero, or Andean Peruvian Shaman. Most spiritual traditions have basic principle they follow. I have found them to be similar, usually stating the same truth just in different ways. I find this actually helpful for a seeker because often when we hear the same truth in a different way we finally understand it.

The principles of the Peruvian Shaman or the seeker of the Beauty way include: Munay, to practice loving kindness and live life in beauty; Yachay, work to develop correct knowledge guided by wisdom; Llank'ay, live with right action, do good work and leave a legacy; Kawsay, respect life and all life-sustaining processes, understanding that there is living energy in all things; and Ayni, the most important principle of all! Ayni teaches that all of life is about appreciation and reciprocity, and that respect and reciprocity are not exclusive to Ceremonies but are to be included in everyday life. Ayni includes the belief that we are to give back in appreciation to humanity, for the benefit of the whole.

Understanding the five principles of the Munay-Ki can add a depth to other principles learned and adopted through other Shamanistic traditions, spiritual truth teachings, or other energetic modalities. A deeper contemplation or study of them can bring a deeper understanding of how to accomplish the goal of self-healing and learning to create our dream from choice rather than family programing or social domestication.

CHAPTER 2

Before the Ceremony

We do not go into Ceremony to talk about God.
We go into Ceremony to talk with God.
– Quanah Parker, Comanche Chief

Prior to doing any healing or Shamanic work use sage to smudge or smoke the area and the participants. Sage is a sacred herb and burning it, then passing the smoke around the outline of the body or around a room will clear the aura or energy field, releasing misaligned energy removing it so it does not affect the ceremony or the healing. When Shamanic or healing work is done, especially ceremony, you are entering the aura or energy field of the participants. It is important to make sure the energy field is clear and no one has brought attached negative energy to the ceremony or healing.

One of the most important things to learn as a healer, energy worker or Shaman is to create a sacred space. A sacred space is a protective area to do healing work or ceremonies. It is created in most energy or healing traditions, even in magic, just in different forms. Although some healers do not create sacred space when they work with the spirit world, those who do, will confirm it makes healing or journey work much more effective, and easier.

The Shaman learns to create a special sacred space to use when healing or performing shamanic work, both for their protection and to allow assistance from the Divine. In sacred space, the ordinary laws of time and space are suspended. It allows Angels, Earth Keepers, or personal guides, who are a higher vibration than humans, a place where they can assist the Shaman to do their work more effectively. You do not have to create a sacred space to do healing work, but when you do, it makes it much more powerful and effective.

The Shaman creates a sacred space for ceremony by calling on the four cardinal directions, and the Earth below, and the Sky above asking them to create a sacred space of protection and lend them their energy for their work. This brings the Shaman into alignment with the spiritual world connecting them to nature by their acknowledgment of the seven fundamental directions. In this way the Shaman aligns with those powers that create and destroy life.

Usually sacred space is created after smudging, by first offering a prayer to the Great Spirit or Universe, then calling to the directions while facing that direction. The Shaman will shake a rattle or hold up a hand toward each of the six directions just prior to or when calling to them to create the sacred space. The Beauty Way is based on the Munay-Ki Peruvian Shamanic tradition of South America, so we begin the process of opening sacred space with the direction of the South. After prayer, turn to the South rattling then calling to the energies of the south. Next move to the West and repeat the process of rattling and calling to the West. Next face the North, then the East, below to the Mother and above to the Father.

It is important to remember to close the sacred space when you are finished doing your journey, drumming, ceremony or healing session. You can do this by thanking each direction in turn, starting with the South. Holding up a hand toward each direction, express your gratitude for their assistance. An ending prayer of gratitude to the Great Spirit or the Universe is also appropriate. Gratitude is what manifests. To be successful in our endeavors as Shaman we must always remember to say thank you for the opportunity to be of service to the Great Divine. In essence, we do nothing. We are just conduits for the Divine Energy.

As a Shaman progresses in their practice, they usually develop their own personal way to open sacred space, and create their own prayers of appreciation. To help the new Shaman begin, we offer this simple example of doing both until you are led by the Great Spirit to speak in your own words.

CREATING SACRED SPACE

Example of a simple opening prayer:
Mother Earth, Father Sky,
Thank you for the beauty and love that surrounds me.
May I bring peace to myself, and everyone I come into contact with
Joy to myself, and everyone I see,
May I walk in beauty, joy and peace.

Here is an example of calling in the directions when creating your sacred space. Use a rattle or drum, sage smoke or just holding up your hand toward the directions when speaking.

To the Winds of the South, come and create a sacred space for us to do our healing work. Help us shed our wounds all at once just as a snake sheds her skin. Come and be with us now. Thank you for creating a sacred space.

To the Winds of the West, come and create a sacred space for us to do our healing work. Help us to be warriors without enemies just like the jaguar, who releases our fear. Come and be with us now. Thank you for creating a sacred space.

To the Winds of the North, come and create a sacred space for us to do our healing work. Like the Hummingbird, help us to make the impossible journey to wholeness. Connect us to the wisdom of the ancestors. Come and be with us now. Thank you for creating a sacred space.

To the Winds of the East, come and create a sacred space for us to do our healing work. Like the great Eagle and Condor, who fly wing to wing with the Great Spirit, allow us to create a new dream. Come and be with us now. Thank you for creating a sacred space.

Mother Earth, you who support, nurture, and sustain us, come and be with us now. We give you our misaligned energy so you in reciprocity will give us prosperity and health. Help us to continue to walk in Beauty. Come and be with us now. Thank you for creating a sacred space.

Father Sun whose light gives life to the whole world, come and be with us now. Give us your life force energy that we may continue to walk in Beauty, that we may be filled with your life force and return to balance, to health and wholeness. Come and be with us now. Thank you for creating a sacred space.

Example of a simple closing prayer:
Infinite Spirit, Divine Oneness, Mother, Father God, Thank you for the opportunity to be of service. We give this situation to you asking only that our hearts are open to give and receive love. In all things we ask for the Divine Design to manifest, that we see clearly your perfect plan and are given the courage to work toward it.

Beauty is before me,
Beauty is behind me,
Beauty is beside me,
I am surrounded in Beauty,
In Beauty I walk.
                    Navaho Prayer

PERSONAL SACRED SPACE

Unique to the Peruvian Shaman is the additional creation of a personal sacred space when doing Shamanic work by expanding or opening the Wiracocha (God as creator), or eighth chakra that resides above the head. This chakra or energy center is considered the soul chakra. The belief is that when you pass from the physical world your spirit draws up to this eighth chakra as a ball of energy before returning to the Divine. It carries with it all our lessons, wounds, and karma. When we re-manifest a physical body for our next incarnation it is created by the stored energy in the energy ball from our eighth chakra.

Opening personal sacred space when doing Shamanic work creates a micro universe out of ordinary time, a place where we can step into infinity. It creates an even more personal protective space to do our work. This personal sacred space is a higher vibration than the energy of the ordinary world allowing our personal helpers, guides, and the Earth Keepers better access to assist and connect with us. If you are doing a healing or a fire ceremony, you may also want to open your personal sacred space or Wiracocha over the client, situation, or fire as well after creating a sacred space for better results.

To create a personal sacred space, after opening the larger sacred space, take your hands from a prayer position at your heart and reach up over head until your arms are straight above you. Your fingers will be inside the eighth chakra or Wiracocha. From there you open your hands out to the sides like a fan, moving your arms down your sides enclosing yourself in a large bubble. You are expanding your soul chakra, your aura, creating a space with a higher vibration around you. It is important to remember to close this personal space when you are finished working by taking your hands back up from the side over your head then bringing them back down to the heart in a prayer position.

FIRE CEREMONY

Many traditions teach a fire ceremony to manifest, purify, or to send prayers to the Divine Source. There are many variations that can be used for different ceremonies of manifestation. After the Beauty Way energetic ceremonial connections, we do a fire ceremony as a way to germinate the seeds of the Munay-Ki helping them begin to grow.

This Shamanic tradition is considered a rapid path to enlightenment, a path of fire, or lightning and the fire ceremony represents this rapid path. It is used to help germinate the seeds that you are gifted during ceremony. This process of germinating the seeds allows your personal healing to come up gently.

Most of the practices of the Peruvian Shaman are agricultural in mind. The sun or fire element represents the way we participate in growing the seeds that are planted in the Luminous Energy Field during ceremony. It is helpful to do a fire ceremony at least once a week in the beginning of your practice. This helps to both release that which no longer serves you, and to grow and expand that which does. Later, standing in the sun and feeding your seeds is just as effective to keep you grounded and moving toward a life in the Beauty Way.

To do a fire ceremony, find a place that is quiet and calm, where you will not be disturbed. Gather something to create a fire. It could be in your fire place, around some candles, outdoors by a bonfire, or even an area where you can sit or stand in the sun. Prepare yourself and the space by smudging whenever possible, but do not be dogmatic about that. Often an impromptu fire ceremony in front of the setting or rising sun can be extremely powerful!

Open Sacred Space calling in the four directions, the Earth below, and the Heavens above. Take a few deep breaths to release the everyday world and drop into the vibration of the sacred. Now light the fire, or sit in the sun, then take a place by the fire, or what you are using to represent a fire. Next, open your personal sacred space. While looking into the fire with a soft gaze, use your hands to draw the energy of the flame into your body. Begin by drawing the energy of fire into your heart to honor the energy of the Beauty Way, or Love.

Next, draw the energy of the fire into your chakras, first by reaching toward the fire then toward each chakra in turn. If you are working on, or just had a particular energetic connection ceremony, feed the seeds you were gifted during that ceremony. You may also add affirmation if it feels right.

As you draw the energy of the fire to your chakras and seeds, pause for a moment and allow the light and warmth of the fire to penetrate into your being. Invite Spirit to germinate the seeds to release their power and beauty. Spend the amount of time that feels appropriate to you. After you have addressed all the chakras in your body, and brought the fire to all the seeds gifted to you, close your personal sacred space, then the large sacred space, say an ending prayer and put out the fire, candles, or let the bonfire burn down naturally.

Here is an example of an ending prayer I like to use. *"Thank you Divine Source for bringing me closer to a deeper understanding and connection to you. Thank you for opening me to my well-being, for manifesting good, joy, and prosperity in my life. I open to your guidance and move toward my good. Allow me to continue to walk in Beauty, to follow the Beauty Way."*

After the fire ceremony, it is a good time to journal your thoughts, or to express them with others that may be doing your ceremony with you. If the ceremony was with a group, we use a stone to pass around the circle so that whoever has the stone is the only one allowed to talk. This gives that person the opportunity to be heard unconditionally and allows people to express themselves or to share their experiences.

At first it may seem somewhat daunting and legalistic to do fire ceremonies, and to always open sacred space when you want to do healing or journey work, but it gets easier and faster with practice. Most people who have done healing work, or sacred ceremony will attest to the amazing amplified results in their work when they begin to honor the directions and open sacred space.

We are not accustomed in the Western world to having to do what we think is a lot of work to get what we want. We like instant gratification. We get tired and bored just as we are about to make a breakthrough, just before completion. We are used to others, the priest, the teacher, the doctor, doing our work for us. The Shamanic path is one of self-responsibility. It is up to us to initiate our own growth and learning through the ceremony. The sacrifice we bring to the altar of learning is our willingness to do the work, the right action of being responsible for our own growth. Take heart, and always hold in the back of your minds, that once the ground work is laid, the seeds are grown, we do not have to keep feeding them as often or so intently.

CHAPTER 3

We Are Made of Elements

*All elements have their source in the Spirit World and therefore are
infused with Spirits that can be contacted for any number of purposes.*
- Lena & Jose Stevens, PH.D

No matter what Shamanic form or healing modality you practice, an understanding of the elements will help you better connect with the Spirit within making all your undertakings more powerful. Before technology, people knew in order to survive they needed to respect the elements and live in harmony with nature. Many of us have forgotten that in today's world. We have forgotten or never realized everything is made of elements. We are made of the elements and can employ their assistance if we become their friends. The five elements are Earth, Water, Fire, Air and Spirit.

All of the elements have both an important lesson for us and also give us assistance in our journey and healing paths. When we study and contemplate the elements we begin to understand their 'personalities'. This can assist us in deciding which element to choose when we would like assistance in our healing work because change can come when we shift elements. We can accomplish different things easier with different elements.

We know which one of our friends will help us with our work, are better play mates, or know how to counsel us when we need it and so it is with the elements once we understand them. They can be used separately to help a Shaman with a specific situation, or can work together for you depending on your need. Understanding what they can do, their basic abilities can be of great assistance for the Shaman in determining which one to use in a situation where they are reprograming energy.

One of the first things a Shaman or energy worker needs to do is create a relationship with the elements: earth, water, fire, air and Spirit – the consciousness within all the elements. All elements are representatives of the One Great Power and by communication and thanking them you are speaking directly to Source. It is through our humility that we grow more powerful, so by showing respect and communicating with the elements around us, we will be able to harness them as allies in a cooperative relationship. When in nature, speak to them, saying, "Good Morning Sun, Hello Brother Rock, Welcome Grandmother Rain, and Thank you Sister Water" whether in your mind or out loud. Later, for the most productive results we learn to let go of resistance and merge with them in ceremony, remembering that in reality we are all made of these elements. They can teach us to be more fully integrated with the powers that surround us, if we ask them. They give us direct knowledge as we learn to work with the elements, the wind or water, the fire or the air.

Elements teach us to be more fully integrated with the powers that surround us and can help us overcome our social programming learning to love the Mother, or nature, more deeply. They can give us direct knowledge as we learn to work with them. Through journey we can understand them better. After contemplating and getting a basic understanding of the elements I encourage people to connect to them through ceremony, a meditation or journey, so they can begin to develop a more personal relationship with them. Read the information about the elements to help remember their basic aspects, then do a ceremony in sacred space to connect to them.

EARTH – Earth is the foundation of all elements. It is the one we are most familiar with but also the element we tend to take for granted the most. It makes up the material world and is the substantial part of our life that we experience through the senses. It represents the practical side of life, our work, our accomplishments, our connections to the physical world. Earth keeps us grounded, a very important thing to learn about when you are working with energy. This grounding ability of earth is the one of the most beneficial things to learn to connect with concerning the element of Earth.

Earth is one of the most important elements to develop a relationship with since everything we do in the physical world is done upon it. It not only rules the most mundane aspects of our lives: working, playing, sleeping, eating, gardening, and raising families but is necessary for life to exist. It rules our foundation, our balance, our ability to persevere, and to focus. It is the manifestation of the idea in the material world. This stable element is the symbol of successful completion and the foundation upon which the future is built. The positive aspects of Earth also include a sense of security, confidence in your own strength, the ability to see the task or situation through to the end, and the ability to focus and concentrate. Earth is the densest element and is home to all the elements. Colors associated with Earth are orange, brown, and tan.

WATER – The element of Water represents the subconscious and the emotional part of our life. The feeling of emotional investment we have in what we are doing. It gives us the ability to access emotional information from our feelings, making wiser choices, helping keep us balanced. In this way it assists the element of Earth. Water is feminine, fertile, flows, and dissolves all hardness. It is mutable which means it can take the shape of whatever contains it.

We are made up of at least seventy percent water mirroring the oceans content on the Earth. We are all born from water in the womb. It is the tides, wells, springs, ponds, rivers, lakes, seas, rain, sleet, snow and hail. It symbolizes purification, the unconscious, our memories and intuition, and the constant change inevitable in life. It is the element of absorption and germination. It is also the perseverance and the courage needed to endure the long gestation of our ideas or desires. Water is nurturing and plays a supporting role throughout our lives. The element of both deep, enduring love, and of the deepest sorrow, it also represents forgotten wisdom held deep in the heart. When you know what to do, but don't know how you know, that too, is Water. Water rules intuition, racial memories, and psychic powers.

When expressed positively, Water emotions are fluid, changing with the demands. They are nurturing and mothering. The changes Water brings are slow in coming but constant, just as the running stream gradually erodes the mountain over time. Colors associated with Water include blue, green, and white.

AIR – The element of Air symbolizes the invisibility of thought. It represents the new idea, the seed of knowledge, and the freedom to choose which direction to move. When contemplating air, think of the wind. Thoughts travel in the air quickly, like the wind.

Air is a connecting element that allows us to perceive things we cannot necessarily see. It is the element of the intellect, the first step towards creation. It is our daydreams, our thoughts blowing free through the recesses of the mind. Our thoughts create our reality. Knowing no constraints, air sends our thought forms into the world to germinate and manifest. Air is also the place to connect with the Enlightened Master Teachers, with Wisdom.

Air symbolizes communications, all intuitive and psychic work. It can be used to develop psychic abilities. It also symbolizes knowledge, abstract learning, theory, transportation, windswept hills, plains, windy beaches, tornadoes, hurricanes, lofty mountain peaks, and high towers. They are all connected with the Element of Air. Associated with knowledge and all matters related to knowledge and learning, it is perception, analytic thought, communication, and memory as well.

Air teaches us the pure, clear, uncluttered visualization that's so important in affecting change. It is also the movement or catalyst that sends our visualization out towards manifestation. We can only survive for a few minutes without Air, the 'Breath of Life'. Colors associated with Air are yellow, blue and white.

FIRE – The element of Fire is elusive and powerful, like life force itself. It is the Fire element that allows us to become invested in the things we do. The passion we generate when we follow our heart. It connects us to the spiritual dimension just like the heart. That is why we are often taught the Fire of life lives within our heart. We all have Fire in our bellies and our hearts. We are human furnaces. We are stars. Fire is that force and ability we have to renew ourselves through spiritual experiences. It is the most primal of elements, connected to our will, passion, and intensity. It is the essence of all processes of change. It is the desire and will to manifest the idea, the driving life force, and the principle of transformation. Fire is also the essence of sex and passion. It is the spark of Divinity which shines within us and in all living things. For this reason, Fire is both the most physical and spiritual of the elements.

The element of Fire is Spirit, light, the Sun, the flame, and the stars. It is the Creative Source of all Light and Life. It is energy, illumination and enlightenment, heat, warmth, protection, active, dynamic, and expansive. It is both healing and destructive, purifying and transforming. Volcanoes, deserts, lightning, eruptions and explosions are all fiery.

Fire is the most active of elements, representing motivation of all sorts including the will to create or to destroy, to move towards something, or just to move for the sake of moving. Fire emotions are intense and urgent, but they usually pass quickly. They include desire, anger, joy, and panic. Without Fire to prod the other elements along, the world would settle into an uninteresting fixed state. Colors associated with Fire are red, yellow, crimson, gold, orange and white.

SPIRIT – The Element of Spirit is the element that transcends all other elements yet is a part of them all. This ethereal element has no direction, yet encompasses all directions. It is the center, the circumference, above and below. It is beyond seasons and time, yet is all seasons and time. It is the realm of the All. It is protection and justice, movement and mastery, life, death and rebirth. It is often symbolized by the turning wheel, or the sign of Infinity. Colors associated with Spirit are Violet, Gold and White.

Knowing that all things are created from and are in essence different combinations or amounts of the different elements, you can use this knowledge in your Shamanic healing work. You can evaluate a client or yourself then reorder the elements in their makeup to assist their shift. Is your client flighty, having a hard time paying attention? More Earth would be helpful. Are they angry or intense? They may have too much Fire element. Adding more water element in their environment or diet could help calm them. Are they having difficulty concentrating or communicating with others? It could be an indication they need more Air element in their life. Someone who is too emotional or sad has too much water element in their life.

How do you reorder the elemental energy in your life? Changing your diet, or aspects of your environment will help. The quickest and most effective way in my mind is to go into ceremony and communicate with the elements asking them for assistance. During an active ceremonial journey you can ask an element to help you. You can ask water to calm you, air to help your remember, earth to ground and protect you, fire to give you more energy. You can ask Spirit to give you the information you need to make the changes to rebalance yourself or your client. But first you must have a relationship, a friendship with the elements.

While writing this book, I had the opportunity to do a journey on the elements then reflect on my revelations with my good friend and fellow Shaman, Neutrina Spirit Walker. Although some of the insights on the elements may seem like a repeat of the information already given, the discussion during our contemplation on the elements gave me such a deep internalization of elemental understanding, I feel compelled to included our thoughts as well in this book.

Earth is restrictive but as so creates a type of protection for Spirit. It holds us in the physical world. Our Spirits are like seeds within it, seeds of possibility. Earth as the body, holds us separate as in separate vessels. We are similar to ocean water in different vessels, separate, but still all ocean water. So it is with our Spirit, we are all the same Atman or Universal Soul but held in different bodies or vessels created by Earth. This is done so we can experience diversity within the Unity of Spirit, so Earth is the host of both Diversity and Unity at the same time. Earth can be said to be both yes and no at the same time, a spiritual paradox, much like the cells in our bodies, separate but part of a whole.

Earth nourishes itself, it nourishes its creations. It nourishes us. It holds all the seeds of life and it expands itself by giving more life to other forms. It grows into grass for animals, food for humans, flowers for birds, bees, and butterflies. This expansion of itself is done as a nourishment and is a perpetuation of itself, of life. We are Earth, and as it is self-perpetuating, so are we.

The planet Earth is a living entity. It recycles itself by transmuting and clearing misaligned energy, patterning it toward the expansion of itself, of life. All things that contain life are recycled back into Earth when the Spirit leaves the Earth vessel, whether that is a body or a tree. Fecal matter, decayed plants, deteriorating flesh, burned wood, all transmute back into Earth or ash, into a space where the seeds of life or energy can begin again to form a vessel to contain Spirit.

Earth supports and is a host to various different life forms, both on top of it and under-ground. Under the ground are diverse bugs, bacteria, worms and other life forms demonstrating a variety of ways life can express itself within the Earth. On top of the Earth are different species as well, various plants and animals all supported and sustained by Earth. Different cultures, different styles, and beliefs are all hosted on top of the Earth. Within, on top, mixed with, and used to contain, Earth creates a space for Spirit to enter into. It is a living entity that gives all other elements a canvas or a space to be and create their unique expression of life. Without it, where would Water pool, what would it soak into, or flow through? Without it what would the

Wind blow upon, move or dance with? Without it, what would Fire consume? Without it what would Spirit use to create its expression of life? Without it, what would sustain or support human life?

Water in all its forms reflects what energy is expressing. Solid (ice), liquid (Water), or gas (steam) all are reflections of energetic movement or possibility. Reflecting on Water's form, we are also able to see how the other elements are interacting with each other.

Water reflects what is being projected upon it, the same as our emotions, which are like Water. They reflect what is within us, what we are projecting out onto our world. Our emotions, like Water, show our disturbances, our wounds, and our joys that are within us. Just as Water moves by the other elements interaction within or upon it, we feel the effects of the energy of emotions that move within us.

Just as we depend on our interaction with our self, in other forms or people, to bring the emotion of love, concern, sharing, caring, anger or fear into creation; it is through interactions with the other elements that Water has movement. Water has no ability to move without outside assistance. It is dependent on the other elements to move it. Earth can allow its gravity to begin Water's flow or stop it. Wind can push Water and move it along, making waves or ripples on its surface. Fire can change Water into steam to float into the atmosphere, or dissipate it completely. Reflecting on human emotions we see this is also true for us. Our feelings and emotions are created or disturbed by our relationship with other people, with outside events, or situations. Emotions by definition mean disturbances.

Water is clear only when it flows or is actively cleaned. If there is no movement, it becomes stagnate and Earth begins to use it for its decaying process. In the same way, our emotions need to flow and be cleared to keep us from becoming ill and stagnant. Water is dependent on movement to keep it clean so it can best perpetuate life. So it is with human emotions, they must flow through us and be cleared for us to keep healthy. It is when they are trapped in the body, held in, frozen like ice or spewed about like steam that they cause us difficulty. Human emotions, like Water are meant to move, and need assistance to do so.

Water seeks itself in an attempt to become a whole unit. Separate little streams flow together, spilled Water will pool. Water is always attempting to work as a 'body' or unit. It is ever attempting to reconnect from the aspect of diversity to the reality of Unity. Water, in its liquid form, can combine with other elements easily, where it unifies, absorbs, and combines to create a whole. Water can mix with all things. This universal solvent both absorbs and dilutes whatever it mixes with eventually becoming one with whatever it is added to.

Water has an almost magnetic draw to itself. This is also true of all humans and all life affected by Water. Animals and plants will group around Water. Human relationships are created around mutual feelings or emotions. Even two drops of Water held close to each other will jump together to connect. How similar this is to human relationships, we are drawn to connect with others. Most are drawn to connect to those with similar emotional needs. Usually people that feel they need to be controlled find those that will control them. Those that have a joyful outlook on life, usually find someone they can express that with. Our relationships show what is within us that causes us to be drawn to them. What we don't like or do like within others, is what we do like or don't like within our self. This is another comment on Water's aspect of reflection and how we as humans are like water.

Although it needs the other elements to move it, Water gives movement to solid things. It can help Earth to change and mutate by softening it, allowing it to travel or have movement. It gives Wind a place to give expression. It calms and dissipates Fire. Boats float on Water, plants and trees are pushed by it, nourished by it, rock is eroded by it, animals and fish move on and within it. Water as an element is also a Divine Paradox, because it can both flow and be still.

Wind is a representation of free will and totally unpredictable. It is not concerned with the outcome of its action. It does not plan, just moves, and does so without permission. It does not discriminate on what or who it blows, but does so with no judgment, worry or concern.

Wind can change from gentle to fierce within a moment. We see Wind from both near and far like the rise or fall of the tide. It is a dancer yet usually dances without pattern. Wind is similar to our words, when suddenly without warning something is said that moves us and shifts us into taking action. Maybe like Wind we could just enjoy the impetus for movement, for dance without purpose. Maybe our constant attempts for purpose are in truth all pointless.

It may serve us to be more like the Wind, to be air with movement, without our need for control, especially the need to control ourselves. To be like the Wind, we may need to let go of all that we allow to control us. When we are trying to control ourselves, we are trying to control the Divine Source within which is both pointless and not in our best interest. To allow ourselves the free movement of Spirit is to have the freedom of both expression and joy.

Wind is an afterthought for most humans. When it comes in force we act surprised. This is also the way it is with our words or communication. We rarely think about what we say, how we say it, or who we say it to. At times we speak like a storm destroying without concern whatever is in our path. At times we speak gently bringing love and empowerment to others. Wind and words are deeply connected just as Water and emotions are connected. Communication can either empower us, and others, or it can cause destruction, just like a Wind storm. Although Wind may seem to empower things to move and shift, that is not its purpose, it does what it does for itself alone. Quite similar to most humans who often speak without concern of the effects.

On contemplation, we see the stress or challenge Wind places on the trees gives them the ability to stand tall. This gives us reason to redefine our judgment, and to consider, how our life challenges and stresses may strengthen us as well.

Fire, the heat from the Sun or Divine Spirit, causes the space between the air molecules to expand. This allows air to move as Wind, showing us that all elements use the others to be empowered, have movement, or shift. They build on each other and use the ones below them as a canvas for expression. They can all exist alone but they cannot have movement or expression without each other, except for Fire. Fire cannot exist alone because it must consume the other elements to exist.

Wind or air also seems to clear and clean itself of impurities as it blows or moves about. It removes Earth and Water from itself through its movements. Wind assists the other elements in their movements and transmutations, or stops them, making it also a Divine Paradox.

I call true spiritual seekers Wind Walkers. Just like Wind, they allow the Divine Purpose to move them without acknowledgement or concern as to who or what is being moved. They dance without purpose. People may see a Wind Walker's effect on others, their environment, or the energy around them, but rarely acknowledge or see them! Like the Wind they are invisible and without warning clear the air! Unlike the Wind, these spiritual seekers are able to keep themselves balanced by choice like a gentle empowering breeze. They are not without the ability to make drastic shifts when needed.

Fire can be chaotic and uncontrollable when out of balance. It transmutes all the other elements through its destruction of them. Although it does create movement in air, it primarily destroys allowing a new creation to develop after doing so. How often the forest regrows healthier after a fire, allowing more room for growth and new life. The destruction of Fire purifies what no longer serves us. Fire's transformation comes from total destruction. Like the 'Phoenix rising' from ashes, because nothing can be reborn until the old is totally destroyed. Fire lives through its destruction and consumption of the other elements. This I find similar to the Western mind set of consumption and survival through destruction. Fire is also a Divine paradox like the other elements. Its ability to allow creation comes from its ability to transform through destruction.

It is interesting to me to note that Fire destroys in the same ratio as its size. A large Fire destroys a large area, while a small candle Fire destroys or consumes a small amount of wax. When balanced, small and contained, Fire is very healing, and protective. It gives light, provides warmth, allowing us survival or life. We can use it to cook and it provides warmth.

An important aspect of Fire or light is that it helps us see within the darkness of the void both literally and symbolically. Without Fire, or light, the other elements would not be known to us. We could not see them, or their effects. Without the heat that separates the molecules, air would not move as Wind, Water would not move but would remain frozen. Without Water in a liquid form, Earth would not soften or be opened to allow the germination of the possibility of life. Fire allows the other elements movement, and gives space through heat for Spirit to move within the elements, within us. Fire seems to be the other side of Earth, its opposite. One is dense the other is spacious.

Fire could be a mystery to us, something we have difficulty understanding because we don't really want to know its aspects completely. We don't want to remember or even contemplate the inevitable destruction of our own form, our own transmutation. We don't want this game of life to be over. We do not want to turn back into Earth to start again. Maybe we are enjoying our movement through the elements so we focus on the vessel we are in, the form that Spirit uses for its movement in space rather than on the Spirit within the form. We don't want to remember that life and energy are ever moving and changing because we do not want this life to ever be over. We don't want to remember that eventually we will start again, as Earth, then Water, then Wind, Fire and another inevitable transmutation.

All four elements complete the cycle of what we as humans call 'life to death'. In truth, there is no death, just a shifting of the movement of Spirit through different elemental forms. Life to death, and death to life is but a pattern of Spirit's movement through the elements. Knowing this could help us understand and release our judgment of circumstances and situations in our personal lives.

Earth expands itself, by creating life. Fire expands itself through destruction and consumption. The creation of Earth from its destruction is a spiritual paradox. Wind and Water move between them communicating between themselves. They do not move or shift because it is right or needs to be done, it is just their cycle, what they do. I wonder if it is possible that we can extend the game through choice by how we flow through the elements of life. We may be able to blow out the Fire or flame of destruction by our choices. As spiritual seekers could we not blow out the drama of disturbances in our lives, liquefy stuck emotions, or just enjoy the movement through life with no judgment or anger? Could we decide to play the game of Wind, go where we will without concern, or the game of Water, to flow or be calm, or the game of Fire, to give light or destroy all around us? We can be Earth, restrict ourselves, or give and nourish all life. It seems as Wind Walkers, spiritual seekers, we can move through the elements either forward or back. We can play life in a different forms, considering whether the form is constructive or destructive to us personally, physically, emotionally, mentally or spiritually. We can choose whether to end the game or not. Our choice seems to be always – yes and no, the opportunity for – both and, for all experiences.

Spirit is the essence of life in all elements. This essence of life is within us as well. Its movement, or ability to transform or transmute is different within different combinations of elements. The less dense an element is the more movement the Spirit seems to have within it. The element Fire gives Spirit the ability to move about more than is possible in other denser elements. Although the density of a combination or element may restrict Spirit, there is no indication of any less life essence in any combination. Density seems to restrict the movement but there is the same potential of life force or Spirit in all things.

Spirit could be the word for a balanced elemental energy that is able to transmute itself as well as to increase or decrease movement within an elemental combination of energy as needed. As an example: when Spirit uses Wind, since air is a lighter element, it goes as it wills. When Spirit works through Water, it flows, soothes, cools, envelopes, shifts between solid, liquid or gas. When Spirit needs to contain, hold, nurture, transmute energy, or create life, it uses Earth. When it needs to transform so there is room for a new creation, it uses Fire.

Working with and understanding elements and how to move through them, both forward and backward is elemental Wind Walking. This is how the Divine Spirit moves through all elements. It is often called the Neutrino or God Particle. Spirit is the Divine particle or Neutrino that moves without being affected by the other particles or the elementals it moves through.

It moves through the elements without being affected by them. We are also this Neutrino, or God particle that travels through all the elements. We can also balance and enjoy our life within the elements as we move through them. We can, with awareness, be unaffected by them or use them as we move through them. This is our life, our dream. We are Spirit enjoying the elements as us.

This Spirit or life force uses the elements to experience, shift and enjoy the game and experience of life. Spirit also uses the elements, and especially Water, to talk to itself and communicate thoughts and feelings. Water seems to be the element Spirit uses as a shift point from the ethereal to the solid state because Water shifts between solid, liquid, and gas. These three aspects of Water reflect our emotions as well, blocked, fluid (in either a disturbed or calm state), and etheric or gas. Spirit uses the element of Air or Wind to move from etheric to transformation. Spirit can use Wind to fan the flames of Fire bringing on a transformation through consumption recreating Earth which then recreates the opportunity for life.

No matter how the elements combine to create, everything is really the same thing. It is an elemental combination filled with life force. The difference between different creations or elemental combinations lies in Spirit's ability to move through the element due to its density.

Although we have been discussing what seems to be a circular pattern of transmutation through a specific order of elements, Spirit has the choice to move as it pleases through the elements and is not limited to a specific order. Since we are also filled with this

Spirit it seems to affirm that we also can choose our movement from one element to the other through choice. Since all healing is about rebalancing energy or Spirit, we can change the elemental combination using the conscious rebalancing of elemental energy for healing! We can consider the aspects of each element and work to add or subtract them within ourselves or a situation for balance as a powerful healing technique.

On further contemplation it seems Spirit may be able to extend a specific life cycle or stop the inevitable transmutation into another cycle of life by turning itself back and choosing to move into a denser element. This concept of free will concerning movement would suggest that Spirit can choose which and how much of each element contains it and for what purpose. Maybe this indicates that we can choose with awareness as well. We can choose to be more flexible, more flowing, less reckless or destructive. That with choice and movement we can and do keep the game going in our lives as well. We could choose not to rush to destruction. Using our feelings (Water) instead of always talking (Wind) we could postpone the inevitable evolution to destruction or transformation (Fire). Choice and the knowing that movement through the elemental energy of a situation is not inevitably one way, could assist us in continuing our life game more successfully, since the inevitable reaching of transmutation could be an ending in the eternal effort to evolve. Since we are also Spirit, Consciousness, knowing or life force, logically we could, with awareness, also return into the element of Earth and contain our shift or transmutation. We do not have to rush to destructive behavior through our Fiery behavior, but could move back to an Earthy stillness. We could at will return to or move to work through Watery emotions, or shift to work through Windy communication. With this back and forth movement we could postpone our thoughtless shift into the consumption of Fire and the inevitable ending or transmutation of our relationships and various life situations. We, as Spirit, could choose to swim, to flow with Water deciding to balance ourselves between the calm and the disturbed aspects of our emotions. We could choose to be free like

31

the Wind, doing as we will then return to Water to consider the feelings and emotional aspects of our choices. We could contain the Fire within us just like a small inflexible Earth container.

If Spirit can choose to move back down from Wind to Water extending the game of its creation, with thought and conscious awareness, we could as well. We are made of Earth, Water, Wind, and Fire, and Spirit is flowing through us. When we are ready to begin again, to play a new life game, we could choose to move up to uncontrolled fire to burn up various aspects that no longer serve us before transmuting. We can choose, or rather the Spirit that lives within can choose, its movement or progression. We can with awareness, see and make conscious choices of elemental balance and magic instead of letting past programing control our choices. Aware that we are Spirit, we can extend the game on the physical level by keeping the elements within us balanced. We can use them for our enjoyment in life, shifting through them as it serves us. And even though on some level there is the inevitable end of the cycle for the Earth body that we as Spirit reside in, with awareness we can purposefully move through the elements that we are by choice.

It should also be considered that the cycle of elements is happening on many levels. This flow of Spirit within the elements is both small and large, personal and within community, all happening around us at once. Spirit is an aspect like everything it resides in, both yes and no. We have our own personal cycles through the elements daily, through our lives, our relationships, just as others do as well. Plants, animals, seasons, and all things are cycling energy or Spirit through various aspects of the elemental combinations that they are. Life is a constant movement of energy flowing through the elements. This makes Spirit also a paradox. It is all encompassing, yet can be divided into small units that are still part of the whole.

Looking at Water (emotions, feelings) and Wind (words and communication) it must be stated again that our thoughts and feelings affect what we create in the solid physical world (Earth). Our Wind and Water create our dream.

The elements are tools of Spirit. It is what Spirit or Consciousness uses to create, to think, and to communicate with itself. Our understanding of them, and our relationship with them allows us a more effective ability to manifest our dream. Knowing that, in truth, we are Spirit moving through the elements, manifesting our dream, whether moving purposely or by just allowing, changes everything!

When we come to the understanding that nothing outside of us will make us safe, or give us what we need or want, but rather everything that we desire is created from the Spirit within us and within the elements, we become Wind Walkers through the elements.

Journey to meet the Elements

Smudge yourself, open sacred space, then personal sacred space. If you have a candle, light it. Pray a short prayer to the Divine, then sitting quietly, relax. Begin by breathing slowly for a while, giving yourself time to get into an altered relaxed state. When ready......

Think of an element. What does it look like.... feel like.... or sound like? Give yourself time to reflect on this..... When you have contemplated these thoughts, ask yourself what qualities you would have if you were that element... For example, would you be fluid, free, or light?.... Would you be dense, or sharp?....Take time to reflect on this, contemplating yourself as the element until you begin to feel you are the element..... Then, in your mind move like the element, merging and becoming the element.... Spend a short time merged and being the element in your mind.... After a short while, ask the element, what it knows that can be helpful to you.... Take a moment to listen, being reflective.....then after a few moments release the element, step away mentally from it, thanking it for any information or thoughts that came to you..... Take a moment to reflect on what just happened......Move on to the next element using the same technique......what it is like, what qualities you would have if you were that element, then contemplating and merge with the element, asking what it knows that could be helpful to you and thanking it for the information and experience. Do this with all the elements: Earth, Water, Fire, Air, and Spirit. When you have finished it is a good idea to write down any thoughts that came to you during your meditation or journey.

This journey or meditation helps you develop a friendship with the elements. As in life, it is our friends that aid and help us, rarely strangers. It will also assist you if you contemplate on how elements relate to each other. For example, it could help you understand or know which element to call on for assistance if you know that both Earth and Water will calm Fire, while Air can increase Fire. It could be helpful if you know that Earth calms and absorbs Water, that Fire can evaporate excessive Water, heat Air, and create Earth. Air can move Water so knowledge can cause emotion. Air can increase Fire so communication can stimulate action.

CHAPTER 4

You Are More than Your Physical Body!

….the human organism is not just a physical structure made up of molecules,
we are electrochemical and electromagnetic beings made up of energy fields.
- Jack Schwarz

Although there are many ways to learn, there are really just three ways to acquire knowledge. The first way is when someone or something else tells you information, like a teacher or friend, or when listening to a lecture or reading information. The second way is through apprenticing, watching and observing what or how others do things then following and copying their examples. The third way to learn truth is through direct knowledge, intuition, or revelation.

A Shaman or anyone wanting to be successful in life would be best served to use all three ways to learn. The more ways you can acquire knowledge, the better your decisions, because the World is what you think it is, what you decide it is. There are no limits in life and your energy flows to create where your attention goes, so to have more knowledge is to have more power to create the life you want by choice instead of default. Let us look at the three ways to learn.

The first way, listening or reading information is the way most people learn in school or at work. Although this is an important way to acquire knowledge, it best serves us if we balance it with prudence. Many take other's opinions accepting their ideas or explanation without consideration of whether what they are being told or shown is in their best interest. In humanity's dream, we are trained to listen to the professional without question. We are trained to sit quietly, and accept what we are taught or told. It would better serve us if we would consider whether what we read or hear is in fact truth and serves us.

The second way we acquire knowledge is through observing what or how others do things, then copying their examples. Sadly, many people do not consider if those they are watching or copying are successful at what they are sharing. They become programed by the watching, and do not even consider the probable outcome as a test for truth. It is always best to watch and learn from those that have been successful, and who have accomplished what you are wanting to learn.

Although watching is one of the most important ways to learn, it is important to look at the big picture to see if what you copy will serve you. I always encourage people to remember a Huna (Hawaiian) Shamanic principle: Effectiveness is the measure of truth. If what someone is telling you, teaching or demonstrating is not effective, find a different teacher. Look at the probable end results, and realize that although innovation is important, more so is successful experience.

The third way to learn truth is through direct knowledge, intuition, or revelation. It comes with being connected to Divine Source and is the most powerful way to acquire knowledge. Direct revelation is where knowledge comes directly from Divine Source or Spirit. Einstein learned this way, most genius and spiritual leaders do as well. This way of learning is available to a Shaman. Direct revelation can come through journey, meditation, from an ability to use the God Brain or frontal lobes. We all have these frontal lobes and the ability to learn through direct revelation if we connect into it.

Enlightenment is a word that is describing life with the frontal lobes activated. It can be accomplished through a near death experience, being hit by lightning, years of deep meditation, or though Shamanic Rites like the Munay-Ki or Reiki.

All humans have four main parts to their brain; the Reptilian, the Mammalian/Limbic, the Neocortex and the Frontal Lobes. Understanding the function of each brain can help us determine what our motivation is, and how to transcend it. Harnessing all our brain potential gives us freedom.

Few people use all their brain potential, yet the Shaman acquires the ability to use all four brains as well as the ability to choose when and which one to use in various situations. This frees them from reacting out of emotions or social convention giving them the ability to use a specific section of the brain as they choose. Each of the four brains is important to our life on planet earth. They all build upon each other, and work together, just as the elements, the directions, and the chakras do. All are symbols of a Unity within the diversity of our lives. When the Shaman learns to access each brain by choice and not just by reaction, it gives the ability to acquire direct revelation from Divine Source. What are the four brains of the human and what are their motivation for activation?

The Reptilian Brain or Brainstem is about self-preservation, both survival and reproduction. This brain is the first one that forms right after our conception. It controls all autonomic functions like breathing, body temperature, and heartbeat. It is the brain of survival and marks time by the intervals between meals. In a crisis, this brain takes over and everything becomes about food and water for a person, when it is in total control people stop hearing and functioning rationally. We know people have difficulty transcending this brain if they are obsessed with their diet. This is the only brain we need to use to actually survive in the world. But life is more than survival, and once we know that, we can use deep breathing to help control this brain. Yoga, T'ai Chi and other breath work are very helpful in transcending the control this brain has over our lives.

The Mammalian or Limbic Brain is about fear, fighting, and fornication. This brain controls the emotions of fight or flight, sex, procreation, and all our fears. Its purpose is safety and preservation. Most people live in this brain and its control over us 'kicks in' when we worry about some possible future need not being met. Depending upon how you perceive a situation, it leaves you with a feeling of abundance or scarcity. It breeds a perceived need for protection. It is the brain of symbolic ritual and ceremony, as well as superstitious belief. Much of society functions from a place of scarcity, fear and adversity due to the inability to transcend this brain. It measures time between deeply satisfying emotional events. Internal stillness and peace of mind quiet this brain making meditation the best way to transcend its control over your life. Ritual and ceremony can also create stillness allowing us to rise above the control this portion of the brain has over us. When we harness this brain we can step beyond fear and scarcity and live in abundance. We can then live in intimacy, love and connection with others. Taking control over this brain also allows us to step beyond the violence we inflict on ourselves and others.

The Neocortex is the brain of logic and is the largest in size of all our brains. It is so large it eventually began to wrinkle and fold to provide more space for it in our skulls. It is the brain of music, science, math, art, poetry, of the abstract. At one time its use was available only to a few individuals. Now we expect everyone to use it. This is the cause and effect brain. It has two halves that are connected, the logical and the intuitive side. Although it is changing in our society now, most people usually access just one side of this brain, keeping them off balance. We can never fully get the benefits of this brain unless we balance both the right and left side. This brain measures time in hours and minutes, because it desires to divide everything into sections to better understand the world. Diversity was created by this brain to make sense of the Unity of all things, to allow us to view the physical world through identifying and labeling it, and to give us the ability to interact with ourselves. This is the brain that is creating your dream flavored by the filters of the first two brains that express our fears and needs. To bring it to stillness and be able to move beyond its control it must be brought out of its clock-time focus, and balance both sides. By understanding that time is really circular, not linear, we transcend the power this brain holds over us as well. This is difficult to do, but becoming an observer and seeing our projections can help. Meditation teaches us to become an observer, allowing us to see our projections. This ability to become an observer is also activated through the Shamanic Rite of the Wisdom Keeper of the Munay-Ki by connecting us with those that have already acquired this ability. When fully awakened and in control of this brain, we can step beyond our mind's control into the knowing that we are Spirit, and move into Universal ethics to experience infinity.

The Frontal Lobes or "God Brain" is near the third eye in the middle of the forehead. At one time only Mystics and Saints could access it. Part of Shamanic work is to step into using this brain. Here time is experienced as a wave, as flowing, as circular rather than linear. Once this brain is activated you are able to live life in a meditation, with the ability to affect change in the world, to affect your personal dream. Since the Shaman affects change from this brain, he or she wants to learn to override the primary functions of the lower brains and move into the frontal lobes. We want to be able to continue to use the other three brains when we need them as well, but we want to develop this "God-Brain" so it can reach down to control the other three allowing us to commune with Spirit and break free of time at will. In the past it would take a near death experience or being hit with lightning to activate this aspect of our brain. This brain can now be activated with the Earth Keeper Rite of the Munay-Ki.

Although time spent in yoga, Tai Chi, meditation and other higher consciousness training can be effective, the Munay-Ki is a quick energetic and effective method to harness the four brains. It is the technology to turn on or awaken all four aspects so we are no longer trapped in the lower brains controlled by our emotional or physical needs. A Shaman is able to choose to move into the God brain to manifest at will, yet also to return to the lower brains as well.

Besides having four main parts to their brain, the human being has an egg-like shape of energy, an electromagnetic field surrounding the body called the aura. Understanding this aura or electromagnetic field is important to any form of energy work, to understanding ourselves as creative beings. The Andean tradition calls it the Luminous Energy Field. It is the heat from your body as it burns the flame of life within you. This aura is proven by science, through photography, and there are people who can actually see auras around humans. The more we are able to clear our aura from misaligned or dense energy, keeping it filled with light energy, the larger it becomes and the more we begin to glow with what the Andeans call the 'rainbow body of light'.

All living things have an aura or energy field around them. It has been said that the Buddha had such a large aura he could be felt three miles away. Have you ever looked very close at your arm or leg when it was fairly dark and seen a red ribbon or a glow close to the skin? This is your etheric double; the innermost layer of your aura's field, and is usually the first part of the aura people learn to see.

The aura is divided into different sections. It is like a rainbow around the body. The etheric double is next to the body and has the same shape as the body. It maintains life by distributing energy throughout the chakra system, or energy vortexes in the body. Connected to it is the emotional body, the part of our aura which stores all our emotions. The body is not healthy if the emotions are not healthy. Connected to the emotional body is the mental body which is divided into two parts: the intellectual and intuitive bands, logic and intuition. Our mind is not really in our brain but in our mental body making our thoughts and attitudes crucial to our health. Connected to this mental body is the causal or spiritual body. It is divided into three parts: the will, the higher knowing, and our connection to the Universe. Everything you have done in the past, whether during this life or previous ones is stored in the spiritual body. These seven sections or bands of your aura correlate to the seven chakras or energy vortexes that distribute energy in the body.

It is important to keep your aura cleared. You may want to smooth it from time to time by holding your hands a few inches from your body and moving them from your head to your feet and then shaking out your hands toward the floor. This gives any misaligned energy to the Earth. She loves misaligned energy and will transmute it. It is important not to ever stroke upward as that is like ruffling a chicken's feathers and can be irritating!

You may also want to learn to smudge yourself with sage smoke on occasion to clear your aura. Smudging is a Native American tradition that uses sage smoke to remove negative energy and stress from the aura that you may have picked up in the world. Always smudge people before a ceremony or Rite to make sure they will not bring in any unwanted energy to the sacred space. Smudging places their being into a 'sacred manner.'

What are Chakras or Energy Vortexes?

In addition to the Aura, we also have a series of energy vortexes that transmits both our life force and outside energy throughout our body. These vortexes appear to be like spinning wheels. When these 'wheels' are open and spinning properly we are healthy both physically and emotionally. When they are blocked or have excessive energy stored in them we become ill or emotionally disturbed. The clearer we can make these chakras, the more we are able to step into becoming 'Homo Luminous' beings with rainbow bodies of light and the healthier we will become both physically and emotionally.

We are beings of light! Light helps us to be healthy and happy. Like plants, we need light to survive, and we need this light to be transmitted effectively up, down and throughout the body by a healthy chakra system. Our personal life force energy resides in the lowest chakra where the body meets the legs, and travels up the chakra system, through the body, and out the crown to connect us with the Universal Source. Sunlight and cosmic energy travel down the body from the head or crown chakra, through the chakra system, and fill us with life force energy going out our feet connecting us with the Earth. We are actually much like a lightning rod connecting the energy between above and below, between the Earth Mother and the Sun Father.

Column breathing is an important and simple way to clear the chakras. Sitting quietly while alternately breathing in the head then out the bottom, then in the bottom and out the head, will gently clear the root chakra which is where our fear resides allowing our higher consciousness to communicate with us. In addition, the other chakras may be cleared by breathing in both the crown, and the root, or the head and the bottom, then exhaling out one of the other seven chakras. This will gently clear them.

A second way to clear the chakras is to take your hand, and touch all your fingers to your thumb to make a beak, or Tai Chi hook. Then pointing this hook toward one of your chakras, circle your wrist, then pull the energy out of the chakras and throw it toward the earth. Make sure to make the circles in a clockwise direction thinking of your body as the face of the clock.

One of the benefits of the Munay-Ki Rites of the Peruvian Shaman is that the seeds of the Peruvian Archetypes are placed in the chakras during the third Rite. As they grow, they begin to clear the psychic sludge built up in the chakras, clearing energy which helps us acquire a rainbow body of light energetically.

There are many wonderful books on the chakra system and I would encourage all spiritual seekers to study them. Here I will only give you a brief summary for a quick and simple understanding.

The first chakra is our support, where the life force or energy resides and is found where the body meets the legs. It deals with survival on a physical level, and being connected to 'our tribe'. In the Munay-Ki it is represented by the Serpent. Serpent connects us to the Earth, the feminine and the collective Mother.

The second chakra is found just below the navel. It is about our relationships to others and to our emotions. It gives us the ability to relate in an open, friendly way in our relationships on all levels. In the Munay-Ki it is represented by the Jaguar. Jaguar connects us to all living things on the planet.

The third chakra is located in the solar plexus area. It is about personal power and self-esteem. It is about the ability to take appropriate action in life. In the Munay-Ki it is represented by the Hummingbird. Hummingbird teaches us to drink deeply from the nectar of life.

The fourth chakra is located at the heart center. It is about compassion, forgiveness and love for both ourselves and others. It is the gateway to the spiritual life. It is represented in the Munay-Ki by the Eagle and the Condor. Eagle and Condor teach us to see from a higher perspective, to open our wings and soar, embracing the gift of vision and clarity.

The fifth chakra is at the throat center. It is about creative expression and personal integrity, standing firm in opposition, speaking your truth, and manifesting our desires on the physical level. It is represented in the Munay-Ki by the Archangel called by the Andeans Huascar, the keeper of the lower world who brings harmony and peace to our unconscious/subconscious mind.

The sixth chakra is located on the forehead, a little higher than and between the eyebrows. It is where we receive guidance and channel or tune into the higher self. It is where we seek the truth for ourselves. It is represented in the Munay-Ki by the Archangel called by the Andeans Quetzalcoatl, the keeper of the middle physical world who brings harmony and order to our lives.

The seventh chakra is the crown chakra on the top of the head and is our connection to the Universe or Divine Source. In the Munay-Ki it is represented by the Archangel called by the Andeans Pachakuti. He connects us to all possibilities, the time to come, to who we are becoming, to step into circular time and recognize what can be changed, before it is born.

The eighth chakra is called the Wiracocha or the Soul Star chakra. It is usually located an arm's length above the head. Wiracocha means 'source of the sacred' or 'foam on the ocean'. When cleared, it will illuminate the Luminous Energy Field. Opening this chakra to envelop us creates a personal sacred space acting as an extra shield against the 'noise' of the outside world. With respectful practice, it creates a place outside of time and space in which the Luminous Beings can meet and work with you.

The ninth chakra is shared by everyone. It is outside of time and space and is considered the gateway to the Spirit realm. Both the eighth and ninth chakras are connected by a luminous cord that a Shaman can learn to travel on and experience the vast expanse of creation.

CHAPTER 5

Power Animals,
Allies and Guides

*Having an animal companion with whom you communicate is
the first step in re-entering that 'time outside of time'.*
- Tom Cowan

Shamanism as a spiritual practice does not require any specific
religious beliefs, but it invariably encourages practitioners to
discover animalism, the ancient world view of our ancestors
that all created things: human, animal, plant, landscapes, elements,
and seasons have an intelligent, communicative life force or Spirit.
As children, most of us had spontaneous Shamanic experiences
accompanied by a strong sense of oneness with the Universe.
These were mystical experiences. Ancient people and Shamanic
practitioners believe that all people have Power Animals and Spirit
Animal Guides, helpers that travel with them on this earthly life. We
may not be aware of them or have connected with them, but they
are there to assist us.

Not everyone who practices Shamanism becomes a Shaman,
but anyone with an interest in and dedication to Shamanic wisdom
can become a Shamanic practitioner, a man or woman who searches
through the darkness of life for a spiritual path that is personal,

creative, life affirming and joyful. At the heart of all Shamanism are the controlled visionary experiences that connect the practitioner with spiritual beings who guide, guard, instruct, and bless life. These spiritual beings include Power Animals, or Spirit Animals.

For many, the search for a spiritual practice is the search for the Soul's path. But search as they may, often the Soul's true journey is hidden just beneath conscious awareness. Many seekers spend years stumbling through personal darkness, searching for their Soul's light, searching for the joy of life. Usually in spite of their efforts, the place, timing, and occasion of enlightenment is deterred by forces greater than their own effort. They come in the form of wrong turns, detours, dead ends, worldly distraction, misplaced advice, lack of support from others, and the unwillingness to make the necessary changes that would lead to a truly spiritual life. Distractions prevent them from finding their path.

Power Animals can help. They can help heal emotional wounds, giving knowledge and strength to stay on the path when things get difficult or confusing. Knowing about and working with Power Animals can be a great benefit and assistance on the path to enlightenment, to personal spiritual growth.

In ancient times, before the first ice age, we are told man did not eat animals for food, but could communicate with them. They lived together assisting each other. After the first ice age animals sacrificed themselves for the survival of humanity and now only special people communicate with animals. However, everyone can still connect with their power or Spirit. Each animal on the planet has a type of medicine or power to help us on the spiritual journey. The energy we will need to learn our lessons. When we connect with them, they will share this knowledge and learning with us. Finding and connecting with your personal Power Animal is another way of direct revelation, of communicating with the Divine Source.

Power Animals have specific attributes and abilities they use to help or teach humans and different Power Animals may come in and out of your life for a certain time period if you need their medicine or energy. Power here means spiritual power that comes from inherent knowledge, information, or wisdom that the Power Animal willingly shares with its human companion.

Many Shamanic teachings believe that we are born with and have nine power or totem animals. They represent the medicine, or personal power you carry on this earth walk, or lifetime, whether we have tapped into the use of this power or not. Medicine refers to anything that improves your connection to the Great Mystery and to all of life. Your personal Power Animals help you learn the lessons you are working on in this life and they share their energy with you to help you become successful. They embody and share the traits and skills you may need to accomplish your tests in life, giving you the energy or tools you may need to reach your goals. Some traditions believe that you have two Spirit Animal Guides with you throughout your life. They help a Shaman travel through the dream or Spirit world keeping them from getting lost during their journey. They assist them in bringing back information and pieces of lost soul for the Shaman or their clients. People may or may not connect with their Spirit Animal guides to do journeying but they are always there. We all have Power Animals and they are easily accessed. They want to help humanity.

A Shaman is able to call upon any animal whose power is needed in the same way they can call upon the different elements. They may call upon the power or medicine of a particular animal when in need of specific talents they possess, or just ask for assistance allowing the Universe to bring the most appropriate animal for that time. Understanding the different attributes of various animals can be of great assistance to the Shamanic healer. The animals may represent stamina (elk) or gentleness (deer) or they may carry spiritual messages (hawk). Each different Power Animal will impart their ability and knowledge to us helping with our spiritual walk if asked. An animal card reading can give a connection and insight on how to handle what we are currently working on as well as show us our Power Animal.

Personally, I have found that the animal whose energy and power you need will come to you even without you asking specifically.

Although we can take the action to call upon the element or the animal for power, usually when we are connected to the Universe, what is right and best for us at the time will come to us. Allowing the Universe to handle things for us, trusting the Divine Source is usually the easiest and best way.

You may learn about one of your Power Animals in various different ways. One way is to ask to be shown your Power Animal in a dream. First set your intention asking to be shown your Power Animal just prior to going to sleep at night. Then drink one half of a glass of water before you go to bed, and then the other half as soon as you awaken. Make sure you have a paper and pencil by the bed so you can notate the dream or revelation as most people will suddenly remember their message after drinking the second half of the glass of water.

Some people have found their Power Animal by having a real animal make itself known to them after asking the Universe to give or show them an animal. A hawk almost lands on the car, or a fox runs out in front of you at the park. If you are not sure if it is a Power Animal for you, ask the Universe again. The animal will give you a sign and you will know. Some people have found their Power Animal by seeing an animal in a photo shortly after asking the Universe to reveal it to them. Finding your Power Animal through photos, or in movies or in song is usually accompanied by an inner knowing. With children, usually it is their favorite animal.

One important reason to know your Power Animal is so you can show them respect. If you honor and respect your Power Animals they will help you, if you do not they will leave. It is often taught that the relationship between the human and Power Animal is one of mutual assistance. The animals need you to assist them by showing them respect. Often you can tell if a person has lost their Power Animals because they are accident prone, or they continually have bad luck. The Shaman usually helps this person reconnect with a Power Animal that can assist them, then reminds them of the need to honor and respect the animal. I often recommend people buy replicas of the animal. Donating time or money to the care of that type of animal, to a shelter, or the zoo are all ways to show respect and honor.

Power Animals are there for us if we choose to connect with them. They help us with our spiritual lessons and help us connect to our destinies. They walk the 'blue road' of Spirit, but they help us live on the 'red road' of the physical world. They help us navigate our soul's true journey through life and they are willing to share their strengths and understanding with us.

In the Andean tradition of Shamanism, each direction is represented by an animal that is called upon when creating sacred space, or when their energy is needed to assist the Shaman in healing work. South is the Serpent. West is the Jaguar. North is the Hummingbird, and the East is the Condor. These different animals represent archetypal energy and are considered the Power Animals of the Peruvian Shamanic Tradition. Everyone has their own personal Power Animals that help with healing or during journey, and through the Munay-Ki Rites we are also able to connect and use the power of the archetypal animals of that tradition as well.

Each of these archetypal animals represents a different energy considered to be one of the organizing principles of the Universe. They are the forces or Energy Beings that are planted as seeds in your chakras during the Harmony Rite of the Munay-Ki. The energy they represent is pure potential and it is your engagement with them that will cause them to grow into the powerful forces that inform and organize your energy centers or chakras. Other Shamanic traditions, like the North American Indians, use other animals to represent the same archetypal energies. The animals vary due to the location of the Shamanic tribes and which animals live in their area, but the energies of the directions themselves are still basically the same in all traditions. So do not be put off by an animal due to your Western programming of what that animal means to you. It is the Universal energy that they represent that you are really working with.

South – Serpent – The Serpent is the archetype of the healer. Serpent represents the primeval connection to the feminine, the essential life force. Placed in the South direction, the Serpent symbolizes knowledge, sexuality and healing. It is perhaps the most universal archetype and has always represented the healing power of nature in many cultures.

The staff of medicine, or caduceus, is formed by two Serpents intertwined around a rod. Moses carried a Serpent staff when he led the Israelites through the desert. In Western mythology a Serpent brought us the fruit of the Tree of Knowledge. In the East it is the coiled snake of our life force energy. The Andean's teach the world Serpent holds the planet together, that the rainbow is a Serpent, rivers are Serpents and the night Serpent is the Milky Way. They honor that the Serpent can travel into the ground, on top of the ground, and into the trees above the ground representing healing on all levels, subconscious, conscious, and super conscious.

On our healing journey, we enter life through the South where we learn to shed our past like a Serpent sheds her skin, all at once. This healing shedding includes the mythology that we were cast out of the Garden, separated from beauty, nature and the Great Spirit, that we can no longer talk to trees or rivers. When we shed that mythology we can again walk with beauty healing ourselves and others. We shed the past as an act of power and of love all at once with the assistance of the Serpent. The knowledge that the Serpent offers us is that of survival on the planet, how to work with the abundance of the Garden, our gift from Divine Source. When we rejected the Serpent as evil we rejected nature, the Earth and all feminine knowing.

A symbol of fertility and sexuality, it symbolizes the essential life force that seeks union and creation. Remember that every cell in our body seeks to divide and procreate. In nature, the ability to produce is the creative principle of the cosmos. We can summon the creative principle from the South by calling on the archetype of Serpent. If you or your client have lost the passion for life, or exhausted personal energy and enthusiasm, connecting with the energies of the South will rekindle the longing for life.

West – Jaguar – The Jaguar is a symbol of the steward of the life force, a luminous Warrior who has no enemies in this world or the next. The Jaguar renews and transforms life. It represents sudden transformation in both life and death. These two energies are the same, that which endures is always changing and renewing itself and that which remains unchanged perishes. Jaguar is the one who knows the way to the world of mystery, teaching us to step beyond fear, violence, and death.

This great cat that leaps between the worlds goes beyond fear and death teaching us the ways of the warrior who no longer has enemies, who no longer has a need for enemies. A warrior who has stepped beyond violence and the need for violence in life. Often it is the violence we do toward ourselves we need the most help with from Jaguar. Jaguar also teaches the ways of impeccability, the way beyond death which is the way back to our ancestors.

When we feel out of balance or in crisis, we can work with Jaguar. It will help us to dismember that which must die in order for the new to be born, as well as how to nurture ourselves. It allows those parts that no longer serve us to die. Jaguar can contain the chaotic spread of a disease, emotional trauma, or a fire through the forest. It can be summoned to assist a dying person to find peace in the chaos of that process. It transforms heavy energies within the luminous energy field and devours the negative emotions of anger, fear, and grief. Jaguar helps us transform misaligned energies into light.

North – Hummingbird – Hummingbird connects us with the teachings of the ancient ways, how to hear the voices of the ancients, of the winds, the ways of nature, and our part in the process of creation. When we come to the North and meet Hummingbird, we step beyond power into the Mystery. To work with the Hummingbird is to begin to think of the kind of world we want our children's children to inherit them begin to work for that through prayer and ceremony. Hummingbird brings us to Spirit, to our place in the council of those who have chosen a destiny that benefits the Earth through personal choices. It helps us make the seemingly impossible journey to our wholeness.

Hummingbird represents the courage required to embark on an epic journey despite tremendous odds. It migrates over long distances, traveling every year from Brazil to Canada. At first glance the Hummingbird would not seem suited for this journey, yet it responds to an ancestral call to embark on this epic flight. When we connect with the Hummingbird, we also hear our ancestral call to connect to the Divine source and find our way, no matter how seemingly impossible. When we embark on an epic life journey, it is good to connect with the energy of the Hummingbird. It helps us make the impossible journey to wholeness.

Once connected to the energies of this archetype, we are often propelled on our own epic journey, eventually connecting us back to our source, where our Spirit began. In that place we find joy in living. When there is not enough time, money or know how for what you are attempting, the Hummingbird can provide the courage and guidance necessary for success.

East – The Condor or Eagle – Condor or Eagle represents the principle of seeing from a higher perspective. The energies of this archetype assist us in finding the guiding vision of our lives by allowing us to see into the past and the future, helping us to know where we came from and who we are becoming. It teaches us to see with the eyes of the heart bringing vision, clarity, and foresight into our lives. Eagle and Condor perceive the entire panorama of life without becoming bogged down in its details. When we connect with the Spirit of the Condor or Eagle we are often able to attain new clarity and insight into our lives. Not an intellectual insight, but rather one into our unique calling. We raise ourselves above our life dilemmas on the wings of Eagle putting our lives in better perspective.

The energy of the Eagle or Condor also allows us to rise above the mundane battles that occupy our lives, and consume our energy and attention. It gives us the 'wings' or ability to soar above our trivial day-by-day struggles and see the higher perspective in the situation. It represents the self-transcending principle in nature. This place of the Condor, of the Eagle, is a place where we learn to look beyond the immediate, where we learn to look to our possible destinies not just the probable one. With the assistance of this East energy, we are able to look for the highest destiny for ourselves and those around us.

When creating sacred space for ceremony, the Earth and the Heavens are called upon for assistance as well as the archetype Power Animals and the four cardinal directions. These two directions of above and below represent the masculine and the feminine principles that live in all of us, aspects we must work to keep balanced daily! It is important for us to understand all the directions we work with so I have included a brief explanation of them as well.

Below - The Earth - The Earth represents the receptive and nurturing principle within the Universe. It responds with feminine energy and principles of life and reciprocity. All life emerges from her and is nurtured by her. Her power is to transmute and renew misaligned energy; spiritual, emotional and physical. The summer leaves turn back into rich soil when in the Earth. The bodies of the ancestors are absorbed back into the earth to become one with the trees. The changing seasons represent the mutable quality of Earth. Yet from this absorption of death, life is renewed. All misaligned Energy given her is transmuted into ordered energy. Just as the trees create our oxygen yet need our out breath of carbon dioxide to live, the Earth also needs our disturbed or misaligned energy to create order, peace, prosperity and beauty.

Above - The Sun and the Stars in the sky are the creative life force, the power of Heaven. They represents the masculine principle of action and energy. The power of Heaven is the unchanging. Ancient peoples observed that while the sky appeared to move in the course of the night and the seasons, the stars themselves were unchanging. The constellations were always in the same relationship with each other. Without the light of the Sun, there is no life on Earth. It is the light and the darkness that create life together, the active and the receptive. In truth they are the same energy, below and above are just two sacred nodes on the circle of the eternal. Even in the story of Genesis, the Earth and the Heavens were one in the beginning. The changing Earth contains the unchanging Heavens within it. The dark womb of space contains the Sun.

Summoning the energies of Heaven and Earth reconnects us with the natural cycles of our lives. It allows us to embrace the Mother who always nurtures us and the Father who will never leave us. Coming home to the primeval Mother and Father is tremendously healing, especially for those with childhood wounds.

Like so many traditions, Shamanism believes that the Soul has three parts. When people die, one part of their Soul, the changing part, returns to the Earth to be reabsorbed into nature and become one with all life. Another part, their power and wisdom, returns to the sacred mountains. The third part is the unchanging aspect that returns to the Sun, to the Heavens. Many of the Shamanic Rites of passage are meant to help one recognize that part of them which returns to the Sun that is perpetual and unchanging.

During the Harmony Rite of the Munay-Ki, energetic seeds representing the archetypal Power Animals are placed in our first four chakras and seeds representing three Luminous Beings or Archangels are placed in the three upper chakras. These seeds work to release the heavy energy and trauma that may be residing and holding on to the edges of our chakras for lifetimes. As the seeds grow, they clear our chakras and help us to come into a relationship with these archetypal energies so they can better help and assist us with their power or medicine.

The three luminous beings or Andean Archangels that are placed in the upper three spiritual centers, are represented by three of the Inka ancestors. Huascar, an Inka king that was betrayed by his brother and killed by the Spanish works to organize our subconscious/unconscious mind. That seed energy is placed into the throat chakra. Quetzalcoatl, the God of intelligence and self-reflection works to organize our conscious mind. That seed energy is placed into the third eye chakra. Pachakuti, the great Inka King represents the super conscious mind, our Christ consciousness. He over-turns space-time and is the connection to all possibilities. That seed energy is placed into the crown chakra.

Huáscar (circa 1502–1532) was the grandson of the Inca King Pachakuti. He is now seen as the keeper of the lower world and works to bring harmony and peace to our unconscious or subconscious mind. He was ruler of the Inca Empire for a brief time after the death of his father Huayna Capac, sometime between 1525 and 1527. When his father died, Huáscar in line for the throne, was in command of the capital city of Cuzco and therefore most of the Inca Empire. However, he soon became embroiled in a brutal civil war with his half-brother Atahualpa, who was in command of the northern city of Quito the second largest city in the Empire. Huáscar raised an army and went after Atahualpa in Quito, but he was repelled in a series of battles. He was defeated and captured outside of Cuzco sometime in mid-1532. The deep divisions created in the Empire during the civil war allowed the Spanish to play one side against another when they arrived. By the time both factions realized that the conquistadors represented a far greater threat than each other, it was too late. In Peru, sympathies are still with Huáscar, considered a victim of both his brother and the Spanish. Their conflict, in concept, represents the ongoing battle between our ego and our spiritual aspiration. The energy of Huascar helps us to stop the chaos that runs rampant in our subconscious.

Quetzalcoatl, by many accounts, was the son of the Sun and Earth Goddess, Coatlicue. He was considered the creator God of humanity and represented duality by nature. Half Air and half Earth, this Feathered Serpent God was one of the most important pre–Hispanic deities. His cult is very ancient. The Northern Indigenous Indian cultures know him as Kokopelli, the main protagonist of many of the major Mesoamerican myths. Quetzalcoatl was said to represent Venus as the morning star, to be the God of intelligence, self-reflection, the primordial God of creation, and a giver of life. He is also credited to be the one that gave maize (corn) to mankind. Quetzalcoatl is considered the keeper of the middle physical world bringing harmony, self-reflection, and order to our lives and our conscious mind.

Pachakuti Inka Yupanqui (or Pachakuteq) was the ninth Sapa Inka (1438-1471/1472) of the Kingdom of Cusco. This ninth Inka King was said to be the son of Inka Viracocha, the creator God of the Inka. This ancestral energy that is placed in the crown chakra now represents the concept or energy of our super conscious mind, the energy that connects us to the time to come, and to who we are becoming. Coming into a relationship with this energy allows us to step into circular time and recognize what can be changed so we can change it before it is born.

The Inka culture also has a belief that a Christ like figure they call Pachakuti will return ushering in a thousand year era or Golden Age of Peace. Inka means 'the illuminated ones'. Pachakuti is not just a single figure but rather represents a time in history when the world will be turned on its axis then set right again, a period of peace, and a Golden Age of a thousand years of peace. Pachakuti also means to step outside of time, to step outside of our history which for us has been one of violence. So to align with the Pachakuti energy means we step out of the ordinary time of violence into a sacred time of peace. It is to learn to live in peace and harmony with the Earth, and all people who honor the Pachamama or the Earth mother.

In the Andean understanding of time, it was believed that long periods were linked by severe events which they called Pachakuti from the Aymara/Quechua word Pacha that means space, time, world or earth, and kuti which means to overturn or turn back. It means the shaker of the earth, the overturning of space-time. It is a millennial moment in which one world ends and another begins, when there is a total transformation of life. This concept and belief in him was so entrenched in Andean life that during his reign, the Inka King, Lord Pachakuti, completely transformed the Inka Empire. His reign expanded the Inka Empire to its greatest expansion. He was a master builder and is credited for either building or improving nearly all of the major Inka monuments, including: Coricancha Sun Temple, Sacsayhuman, Pisac, Ollantaytambo and Machu Picchu.

In summary, the four organizing principles are: **Serpent** who connects us to the Earth, the feminine and the collective Mother and helps us to shed our wounds. It resides in the first chakra and represents the direction of the South. **Jaguar** who connects us to all living things on the planet, nurtures us, and teaches us to be warriors without enemies. It resides in the second chakra and represents the direction of the West. **Hummingbird** who teaches us to make the impossible journey, and to learn from the ancestors. It resides in the third chakra and represents the direction of the North. **Eagle/Condor** who teaches us to embrace the gift of vision and clarity, to create our own dream. It resides in the fourth chakra and represents the direction of the East.

The three luminous beings or Andean Archangels are represented by: **Huascar,** the keeper of the lower world who brings harmony and peace to our subconscious mind and resides in the throat chakra. **Quetzalcoatl,** the keeper of the middle physical world who brings harmony and order to our present lives and resides in the third eye. **Pachakuti** who connects us to the time to come, and to who we are becoming. He allows us to step into circular time and recognize what can be changed before it is born. This energy resides in the crown chakra.

The Munay-Ki teachings tell us that now is the time to actively participate in our own evolution, to consciously take the quantum leap we believe is available to us during this present time of acceleration. This participation is accomplished quickly with the help of the nine Rites of the Munay-Ki. Our negative baggage has continued to claim our present reality by its organizing influence creating our reality dream from our past wounds. When our energy field patterns are cleansed and cleared and we are able to observe and heal our wounds, we become available to our destiny. It is then we begin to be influenced not by our past, but by our future, and the possibilities available to us. Cleared from the filters of our wounds we begin to dream our world from choice actively creating our own reality.

CHAPTER 6

Becoming the Seer

Shaman can 'see' in ways not thought possible in society.
- Dolfyn

Throughout most mystical traditions there are references to individuals who can perceive the Luminous Energy Field or the aura. To learn to sense the Luminous Energy Field is an aspect of being a Seer. To do so you must practice. Perceiving or seeing the aura can be learned even by those that have not had the Seer Rite, so I have included exercises later in this chapter to use if you are interested in beginning to see energy.

To be a Seer is to walk softly on the earth dreaming our destiny into being. It is to see with the Shaman's way of seeing, being open to seeing our projections and our wounds, to perceive everything even what others claim is not there. This way we learn to be the one who observes, not identifying with what is seen, but to be self-referencing, identifying with the self. We must be open to see even what we thought was not there within ourselves. Then, as that Seer, we begin to understand things we did not know about ourselves and the world. It is then the world becomes a blank canvas and we can dream whatever we choose to create into being.

The Seer Rite of the Munay-Ki gives us the ability to see from the Shaman's way of seeing. This helps us to track the original wound that caused an imprint in the Luminous Energy Field. Everyone has an original wound that affects their life. This wound is what has colored and informed our current life dream. This Shaman's way of seeing also assists the Shaman to track intrusive energies in the body detecting possible reasons that may be the cause of the emotional or physical difficulties for a client or themselves.

The Shaman's way of seeing is a talent that must be developed. The invisible world cannot be seen with the eyes of logic and reason. Vision is a rather miraculous process. All seeing actually happens inside the head although it appears that we see the world outside with our eyes alone. The eyes are of little use for perceiving the invisible world of energy and spirit. To perceive the aura with its encoded stories we use the visual cortex to do what it is designed it do, create images, but change the source of the signal. We all have the sensors we need to develop the Shaman's way of seeing, the sixth chakra or mythical third eye in the center of our forehead, and the fourth chakra or the heart center. If we connect the heart chakra and the third eye to the visual cortex, we can begin to see the world differently, we see with the Shaman's way.

The Kawak or fourth Rite of the Munay-Ki creates 'cords' to connect the third eye and the heart to the visual cortex allowing us to begin to perceive the world from these chakras instead of just from our projections. It rewires our vision allowing us to choose to use the heart and the third eye when we want to perceive energy.

Everything that you experience mirrors a part of you. Yet we are not confident enough in that thought to explore it in depth. Most of us are unaware that we've been dreaming and that we might envision something else that is uniquely ours. When you change how you perceive reality, you change your dream. When you are able to 'see' your own projections and filters you understand how you are already dreaming your world. You realize you don't have to participate in the dream of society that tells us the purpose of everyone's life is to be obedient to authority. As a Seer you can choose to reject the nightmare that's presented to you by the media and the people around you, then you can recreate your dream your way through choice.

In truth, there is no objective reality because our prophecies are self-fulfilling. The Universe responds to us by meeting our expectations. This is dreaming. The Universe always mirrors back to us the conditions of our dreaming. If we are fearful that money won't come to us, it won't. To be aware of the dream is to learn that where ever we go, there we are. This is a spiritual truth. Once we begin to 'see' differently we are free to choose our beliefs, our mental state and our emotions in every circumstance. We are no longer tied to creating from our old programming of disempowering beliefs. We come to understand that the world is what we think it is, so we can decide what we want.

Our current waking dream is created by our story. The story is what we tell ourselves or others, the narrative we wrap around a particular emotion that we hold. These emotions direct our belief and reality. When we are aware of our waking dreams we can apply the same analytical approach to examining them as we do to our night dreams. Every symbol in your night dream represents a part of you in psychoanalysis. We apply this to our waking dream as well. Everything that happens, that you see, that is around you, is about you. What we see around us is what we have projected. To change the dream and heal, we change our own perception of a situation, or alter our belief, thereby altering our projections.

To become a Seer is to become an observer. It is then we are able to observe what we are doing yet be unaffected by it. As an observer, we can stop judging our thoughts and actions, and instead ask ourselves, "What is the emotion this story is wrapped around? What could this situation be showing me about my own belief in myself or others? What part of me is in this person or action that I don't like?" These questions and those like them will help us identify our stories. Then we begin to see that every part of the story or dream, like in our sleeping dreams, represents us.

Our lives become simpler if we are not weighed down by the baggage of our stories and expectations. We can come into what is called in Buddhism 'beginner's mind'. There we are able to let go of what we believe something is and become open to what it could also be. This is not saying we forget about our years of experience, but rather we stop confusing what we learned yesterday with what we may be discovering today. This observing, the understanding that all we see is a reflection of our own projections develops a more hypothetical relationship with life instead of a fixed one. We are able to stop assuming the outcome in a situation we've been in before, because to assume the outcome, makes it self-fulfilling. Now as the observer we allow ourselves to see the other aspects of our situations. In truth, all possibilities and all realities are there simultaneously.

We have been creating our dream or reality from specific possibilities because our psyche is trying to tell us something. It is trying to motivate us to find closure with our wounds created by specific beliefs. "I am afraid, I don't feel safe, I deserve to be rejected..." all represent beliefs surrounding our wounds. The psyche will not stop trying to get our attention until these beliefs are acknowledged. Once we 'see' them, they can be changed and replaced with a more self-empowering belief. Then we can live a situation from a different possibility.

Observing the same old situations with an open mind, the beginners mind, the situation becomes something new. Now that same argument we have about money with our spouse is seen differently. We can see what is really being expressed in the argument is the wrappings of fear. You are both scared. Once you see this emotion, you observe it, search out the wound, the belief that you hold about money that causes you to project it on to others, and then you make the choice to believe differently, releasing the negative emotion and healing the wound that is the cause of the projection. Remember, if your beliefs don't serve you, change them, you have that right and ability to do that.

As a Seer, we can observe our boss's arrogance 'seeing' that it is really his insecurity about power and importance that makes him act the way he does toward us. Then realizing it is coming from his wounds, we don't have to take it personally anymore. When we see a teen dressed in baggy clothes with hair hiding the face, we see it as the fear of rejection playing out. We see they are creating the opportunity of rejections because they fear rejection.

All people, all of us, create situations for ourselves to reinforce our beliefs, be they lack, or powerlessness, or rejection. Now as a Seer we can choose to see things differently by realizing things are not happening to you, you are creating them. You are drawing them to you, and knowing that, you can clear your vision and make a change in your reality or dream. It becomes a matter of choice.

To be an effective Seer, you must practice integrity by being true to your word. Nothing is more important to the Shaman than being true to their word. You must begin to be very careful about what you say to yourself and to others. Your word is your power to create your reality. Living true to your word builds a spiritual power that is essential if you wish to dream a better world for yourself. It builds up reserves of personal power. The practice of integrity also requires we own our mistakes, correcting them and making amends. Do not be afraid to say you made a mistake. Own up to it, and try again. This is about forgiveness. Forgive yourself. If someone will not forgive you for your mistake, observe the projection and ask what the emotion or wound is that will not allow you to forgive you. There is really only one person here. We just may not quite see it yet!

Among the Inka, Seers were known as the Kawak. In the Nazca plains in the southern desert of Peru, legend says there is an abandoned city known as Kawachi, the 'place of the Seers'. It is an entire town that was dedicated to training individuals to sense the luminous nature of life. The fourth 'Kawak' Rite of the Munay-Ki installs the filaments of light that connects the heart to the visual cortex from the back of the brain to the heart awakening our ability to see the invisible world. It also awakens the 'second attention' allowing us to perceive the luminous side of life perceiving everything to be alive. It opens our eyes to the Shaman's way of seeing.

The Seer Rite allows us begin to see the energy around us and to look at those parts of our self that we have previously not seen or wanted to see. After this Rite we begin to reveal ourselves completely to ourselves. The Seer becomes the witness, the one that all wisdom traditions teach about. This witness, by observing our world, changes it. Some may not actually see auras, but what everyone will begin to see is much more important to personal healing and growth, thier own projections, and those of others.

The Seer Rite moves us out of the primitive aspects of the physical (Serpent) and mental (Jaguar), through the realm of the soul (Hummingbird), and into the spirit level (Eagle) where we can 'see' the beliefs that have created our dream. Once we see them, we can choose to keep or alter them. 'Seeing' our programming, allows us to understand where it came from. We are then able to choose whether we keep or reject the dream that society presents to us. Our life or dream is then no longer created by default, but by choose. Using the techniques of the 'second attention' or observer, observing our story without judgment, we change our dream. Similar to how electrons in quantum physics change with observation and expectation. This most important Rite begins the process of actually giving us the ability to change our personal dream.

Here is an important exercise for those wanting to see energy.

Start by tapping the thymus in the center of your chest, just above the heart a few times. Then close your eyes moving them without moving your head from left to right, up to down, upper left to lower right, and upper right to lower left. Now rotate your eyes in a big circle, left to right three times and then right to left three times. Repeat the eye rotating in small circles. Keep your eyelids shut through the whole exercise.

Bring your hands together in the prayer pose, finger tips touching with space between fingers and palms, hands resting against chest. Take a few deep breaths. Next, separate your hands gently and shake them vigorously from side to side for thirty seconds, relaxing and allowing them to become limp.

Again bring the hands together in prayer pose. Gradually separate your palms but keeping your fingertips together. Be aware of the feeling in your hands. Now finish separating your hands completely and slowly, remaining aware of your fingertips. Next with the fingertips of both hands tap the center of your chest at the level of your heart. Tap the outline of an imaginary necklace of light going from your heart chakra up the neck to the back of your skull, to the visual cortex. Repeat this movement slowly and mindfully three or four times. Next tap on your sixth chakra, the center of your forehead. Tap an imaginary band or line from your forehead around the skull to the base of your skull in the back of the head, like the outline of a headband. Next, tap following a line from the third eye around just above each ear. Repeat several times. Now tap once again on your sixth chakra and follow a line along the top of your head tapping with both hands along the midline to the base of the skull. Imagine that you are placing a crown of light over your head.

To end, take a deep breath, then while visualizing the energy running through the pathways you have created with your tapping, the Crown of Light and the Necklace of Light, exhale with force out the mouth to activate them. In your mind see energy begin to flow on them, connecting both your third eye, and your heart to the visual cortex area at the base of your skull.

CHAPTER 7

Looking at the Mesa,
the Sacred Altar

The mesa is about remembering your personal power.
- Fredy "Puma" Quispe Singona

The Munay-Ki Peruvian tradition, like all Shamanic traditions, is an animistic tradition. It teaches a philosophy that everything is alive, that life energy permeates even rocks, rivers, and trees. Their belief includes the thought that we have a relationship to everything that is alive, even to the environment. Anima is Latin for Soul, and the Shaman sees all life as part of the Great Soul. This concept makes everything sacred. To the Shaman, the Earth and every place on her are sacred. Although some places are more powerful than others, all places on the Earth are sacred because they imbue life force energy.

The task of the Shaman is to establish a relationship with life and the light or luminous threads that connect us to life. All Shamanic traditions as well as religious groups connect to the Divine, this life source, through ceremony in sacred spaces. The Shaman of the Munay-Ki connects to this life source or Divine energy through their mesa, or altar. It is a symbol that represents their connection to the Universe. The mesa altar is similar to the medicine wheel of North

America. It is similar to the ancient altars found by archeologists around the world. Mesa means altar or table. There are mesas or sacred altars that go back into ancient times with their objects of power being handed down from teacher to students.

The Shaman of the Andean tradition lived high in the mountains traveling to their clients. Since their mesa was their connection to power, they would carry them where ever they were needed. The mesa is usually a cloth bundle that is used to carry power objects to healings or ceremony. When the Shaman wants to do a healing or divination, they set the bundle down on the ground, opening it up to create an altar. They then use their special rocks or power objects to mark the directions of North, South, East and West. They may also display other special power objects or tools they have acquired. These power objects often also represent the directional power animals the Shaman can call on for assistance.

Many people create their own home altars for meditation or reflection filled with things that represent abstract thoughts and beliefs. A Shaman's mesa is different. The mesa is a traveling altar with personal power objects that can be used for healing and divination, not a stationary altar with objects that represent abstract thoughts and beliefs. The power objects in a mesa actually energetically connect the Shaman to places of power, archetypal energies, or the healing of a past wound whose energy is now available for positive use in their work.

The rocks or power objects in a Shaman's mesa also may have energetic connections to either the Shaman's teachers or to psychic connections. The objects connecting them to their masters or teachers are usually placed on the right side of the mesa. The objects with 'magical' or psychic energy connections are usually placed on the left side of the mesa. The mesa's power objects can also represent a healed wound (left side) or a way to communicate with an ancient altar or master/teacher (right side). Other stones that connect the Shaman with the foundations or archetypes they are connected to are also placed in different directions on the mesa. Each mesa is unique to each Shaman and can contain many or just a few power objects.

The objects of power in the mesa or traveling altar represent the parts of the Shaman that have healed, wounded parts that in the process of healing now become sources of power. The stones or objects of power that represent the healing or revelations are usually found in a place where that healing happened or an understanding was acquired. They contain the power received in the transformation so that what was once debilitating and disempowering can be used as personal power sources. The power is placed in the object by the Shaman.

The objects as reminders also enable the Shaman to relate and empathize with others in similar situations. They use the objects to connect them to the energy of healing from the power place they came from. This is why we consider the Munay-Ki as first a system of self-healing, because as you learn to heal yourself, then and only then can you truly help others heal as well.

Traditionally to gain objects of power a Shaman traveled to a place of power, the mountain, a special church, or a sacred river to do ceremony. Although this is still the most used way, in today's world power objects can be acquired from any place where you have a deep revelation or a deep connection to the Earth or the Heavens. They can be found where ever you have one of those 'ah ha' moments about your own life. They are usually a gift from nature, given to you after having a revelation about your own dream. They can be given to you by friends or strangers, or teachers as well. These objects become power objects for you because the revelation, the knowing, is transferred to the object and later you are able to connect to the knowing they represent.

Often ancient sites are seen as just archeological ruins to most people, but to engage in ceremony there makes them places of power to the Shaman. There they find objects of power that later enable them to connect to or become the archetypes accessing the energy of the holy mountain, or the rivers where they performed ceremony. The objects energetically connect the Shaman to the power of the sacred places or the energy and abilities of teachers who gave you the object.

Many students on the Shamanic path receive a key stone from their teacher or mentor that becomes the center of their mesa. This key stone connects them to the place where their teacher received Rites of passage, Rites of transmission, or became medicine people. This key stone then becomes an organizing principle in the mesa organizing the Shaman's relationship to knowledge or power. The Pi stone given to a student taking the Munay-Ki Rites usually becomes this center, the key stone object of their mesa. From there they find and add objects of power to their mesa themselves, most of which will come to represent the archetypes of the four directions, the Earth and the Heavens. They will come to represent the lessons that each of the directions teach: to shed our wounds, to release fear, to learn the ancient teachings, to see clearly with vision, to love and give back to the life giving energy of the Earth and to access the life energy of the Sun and Stars. Most power objects revolve around the healing of personal wounds, in relation to these concepts, as well as the wounds of our ancestors. Working with a mesa the Shaman can become an access point to the matrix of creation, release the Luminous Energy Field from time, and no longer be affected only by the past. The opportunity to be influenced by the result of a future destiny becomes possible.

Although the power objects can connect us to power, we have to use this power. To be healed, one must act on their revelations. In truth, we are the gateways or portals to connect to Divine Source, the objects just hold that knowing to remind us of that truth. The Shaman or the client has to take the action to make changes that heal their wounds. For example, once you know you choose unavailable relationships due to your wounds, you can stop and reevaluate your new relationships before you begin to form an attachment. You can choose differently. You can choose a relationship for a new reason, not from an old pattern that no longer serves you. You can choose to stop the negative behavior.

In the healing tradition of the Shaman, the mesa represents the cosmos and how the Shaman engages with the cosmos. When the Shaman opens the mesa, they engage in ceremony. It is then during ceremony that the symbolic objects are used as objects of power. A stone is just a stone until engaged in ceremony. Objects of power used for healing become power objects when engaged in ceremony. This is true of all religions, spiritual practices, and even in magic. An example from other traditions is a Navaho healer that makes a sand painting as a representation of the client, and then by changing the painting, energetically changes the situation or person. They create the symbol then change it into an object of power for use in healing. The Christian Eucharist is also an example of power awakening during ceremony.

In the process of building a mesa the student of Shamanism re-establishes their relationship to nature. They learn to walk in beauty again, to shed old myths. It becomes a process of acquiring power to use for your benefit and the benefit of those you choose to help. The Shaman does not confuse the form of the mesa with the essence of the mesa. The mesa and what it represents is not about superstitions, it is about engaging in personal power, about following the energetic threads to possibility. It is using acquired power objects to come into alignment with Divine Source, the one power and presence. A mesa is a personal power bundle for the Shaman.

Before a ceremony or healing when the Shaman opens their mesa to engage power directly, they first feed the mesa. The basis of the Shaman's relationship with the Universe is one of reciprocity, a continual give or take, so to give back to the Universe or Divine Source in respect for what was given, they symbolically feed their power objects. The Shaman breathes on the objects or sprinkles them with floral essence to awaken them while saying a prayer. The breath is essential because the breath is life. It is a physical act of respect and appreciation. The Soul enters and leaves the body with breath. To breathe on power objects symbolizes waking them, giving them life. Most spiritual traditions, even western religious traditions understand the concept of Ayni, to get you must give. For the Shaman working with a mesa for healing and understanding, it is the breath given, or blown on the power objects that is the exchange of energy needed to receive the stored power.

There are four main directions of the mesa divided into two fields with the Earth and the Sun residing along the center axis. The right side of the mesa is considered the physical, the field of justice, or the way of the healer and sage. The left side is the side of magic and the mystical, the way of the mystic. Within these two sides to the Shaman's mesa are the three elements to knowledge: what can be known, what we know we don't know, and the vast majority – what we don't know we don't know. In the medicine traditions they are also thought of as: what can be known but not told, what cannot be known but experienced – the great mystery, and the basis of the Shamanic belief which is the experience of that which can never be known.

Usually when the mesa cloth is opened and set out, one of the corners of the cloth is facing you, creating a vertical axis. This is the South direction. You do not need to actually be sitting in the South, but rather the corner in front of you is the place that is a representation of the South. This is where you come to heal yourself, to shed your past as an act of love and power. This is where you place the stones that represent your gained power or aspect of the wounded healer. The old wounds now recognized, their memory placed in objects, can be used as power in understanding others that may have the same wounds, or as a reminder of how to release the wounds if or when they come up again in new situations in your own life.

In the West, or to the left, the Shaman places the objects of power that helps them remember how they stepped beyond violence and anger. Those objects in that corner of the cloth help keep fear and violence from being an operating principle in their life. Violence is an aspect of fear. When we are fearful we react with anger and violence. Sadly, most people are not usually violent to those they dislike but against those they love and against themselves. So the task of the medicine person is to learn to step beyond anger, beyond violence, to be warriors without enemies.

The North or the top of the mesa cloth holds the objects of power that assist the Shaman in accessing the mystic domain, those things that become gateways to the other realms and ancient teachings.

These teachings help them step between the worlds and access the knowledge that is timeless, that exists outside of time. The task of the Shaman in the North is to align vision and intent so the Universe begins to actively work for their benefit accomplishing their intent. When the Shaman is aligned with the North, the Universe does not just assist them, but actually conspires to make struggle no longer a factor in their existence.

The East is to your right. In that corner of the mesa the Shaman creates a new dream by envisioning the possible. They dream about what they can become, not what is probable, but the possibilities that they can choose from. The task here is to sit in meditation and create the dream of humanity, a vision for the highest and most holy good, to call forth and create the best destiny for themselves and the world. The power objects kept there help them to dream a new dream for their lives and that of their clients. These objects remind them of times they spontaneously created a better dream, or manifested possibility. It is in this remembering that the template for possibility is open to be used again.

The center of the mesa is both the Earth and the Sun, and can have objects of power that would represent going into the Earth, or reaching for the life energy of the Sun. It represents the silver cord the Shaman may travel on to access either the subconscious or the higher consciousness during journey. A Shaman travels below for assistance and information with the power animals or guides, to clear the past, and to retrieve lost soul parts. They travel above to connect to angelic guides and to access the future possibilities. This center space is often where the Pi stone is placed as it represents the entrance to the other worlds.

As objects of power come to the Shaman they are placed in cloth bags and kept in the mesa bundle. Special power rocks for each direction may be kept in separate bags as well. During a healing or ceremony, or when needing information from the Universe the Shaman takes these power objects out of the bags and places them at one of the directions on the mesa. When the mesa is opened, the Shaman lays them out after breathing into them, connecting with them, and then asking for their wisdom. The Shaman keeps their mesa bundled up until conducting a ceremony or healing session. Opening the mesa allows the Shaman to use the energetic connection or lines that each stone or power object connects them to for assistance in the healing or reading.

When the Shaman acquires power objects, they connect with them by holding them at either the heart chakra or the second chakra, then opening to them in meditation. Then after thanking them for their presence and power, they feel and listen to them. They then ask them what they can teach them, or if they have a story that can help them. The objects can then be programmed to work with the Shaman in healing work or to remind them of the feeling of power and freedom gained from the insight they had just prior to finding it. This is done by asking. Ask and you will receive.

To program a stone or power object, after connecting to it, hold it in the right or giving hand and tell it what you want it to do for you. If you want to receive information, hold it in the left or receiving hand. Remember to say 'thank you' when you are finished. If you can, leave a small offering of exchange when you collect power objects, some sage, tobacco, hair, a song, or at least a heartfelt 'thank you'. Power objects are usually smudged when they are new, or after they have been used to clear and reset their energy. Holding them under flowing water, or placing them in the ground for a while also clears them when necessary.

In this tradition it doesn't matter what the power objects or stones are made of, but rather their shape is what is important. Stones do not have to be gem quality crystals, or even crystals at all when using them in the mesa. Any stone that calls to you after a revelation, or a time in nature can be used as a power object in this tradition.

Smooth stones of any shape composed of obvious layers, especially circular ones are good meditation stones. It will ground or center anyone with excessive disharmonious energy. Holding it, release your Hucha or disorganized energy into the stone, or run it through a person's energy field to draw out their Hucha. To cleanse the object, rinse it in water or touch it to the Earth to release the Hucha from the stone.

Stones with a natural hole all the way through are powerful guardians and teaching stones that may hold powerful secrets revealing many of the mysteries of life. They can be used as a dreaming stone as well, allowing a powerful dream or desire to slip through the hole into consciousness to manifest in the physical.

Stones with square or rectangular lines are doorway stones to help us shift to higher levels of awareness, refine our perceptions, manifest new possibilities, release resistance, and allow blocked energy to flow freely again.

A stone that has three almost identical markings, three protrusions, three doorway lines, three layers and such, is a three world stone. It is used to harmonize our abilities to work with the energies of the three worlds: the lower, middle and higher worlds or the subconscious, conscious, and super conscious mind. These types of stones also harmonize the three main principles of the Munay-Ki: Munay (love), Llank'ay (work and strength of will), and Yachay (wisdom grounded in experience). They help harmonize our abilities in these areas of life.

A triangle stone mystically connects the Shaman to the Apus or Mountain Spirits. It is especially powerful if discovered in the mountains. It can also be a three world stone balancing the three aspects of the mind.

A stone with a face in it, whether human or other, can be a teaching stone or a guardian stone. It can provide specific instruction or protections.

A stone with spirals, circular projections or protrusions are often used as charging or clearing stones. They can be used to increase positive energy or clear misaligned energy from the energy body. Often called Chumpi stones, these stones can have natural projections and are often gathered from the Urubamba River. Chumpi stones are often carved by local artisans usually from either meteorites or alabaster. The stones can be different sizes and often have detailed etchings of the sun, serpents, and cocoa leaves and are often used in sacred ceremonies.

Besides healing, another use of the mesa is divination. Divination is a way of finding information concerning a problem or looking into the future. One way to do a divination with the mesa is by asking questions concerning a problem or situation while circling around the directions on the mesa. The Shaman first sets an intention then beginning in the South connects with the stones or power objects there and asks, "What needs to be shed or healed concerning this situation? What is the problem or wound here?" Contemplating, discussing and reflecting on this for a while. Then moving on to the West, connects and asks, "What needs to die in this situation?" or "What needs to be different? What fear or aspect of violence do I need to release?" After reflecting on the questions move on to the North. In the North, after connecting to the power objects asks, "What needs to be born or reborn? What technique could shift this situation? How do my ancestors fit into this situation? What could help me make this seemingly impossible journey to healing this wound or solving this problem?" After thought and reflection, moving to the East asks, "What do I need to see to shift this? What would this look like from a higher perspective? What is possible, if I shed, release, and choose differently? What are my possibilities?"

The Earth and the Sun may also be asked questions. The Earth may be asked, "What do I need to do to regain my balance, to get grounded? What do I need to offer to the Universe in reciprocity?" or "What do I need to clear from my life?" The Sun can be asked questions like, "What do I need to do to bring more life energy or light into my life, into this situation?" Usually each question shifts or helps clarify the answer to the previous one. So if you don't receive an answer move to the next direction. After circling the mesa in this manner, the possibility of change and the belief that needs to shift or be released usually comes to mind. It is also important to note that the circle goes all ways. It is very appropriate to start at any direction and move in either direction. Sometimes, moving forward and then back to a direction will help the mind receive an answer, or understand the answer it was given. Sometimes I will start in the direction I already know the answer to, like what the violence in a situation is, and move from there.

In summary, to use the mesa for divination, look at the problem in the South. Look at what needs to be released, or let go of in the West, contemplate what fear is causing the situation. In the North consider what techniques we could use, what knowledge remembered will help the situation or how the ancestors could be involved. In the East consider possibilities, what could be possible if changes or shifts in beliefs were made. When aligning or sitting in contemplation with the Earth, consider what to do to clear energy and what to offer as reciprocity for our shift. This is the place to journey to the past, or subconscious to find the wounds that caused the problem. Then with the Sun, ask for energy, for a connection to the Divine Light for assistance. This is the place to journey to the future to find a possible future destiny.

A Medicine person works to come into a relationship of Ayni or reciprocity with the Universe, a relationship that involves something done mutually or in return. When we begin to live from an attitude of Ayni, our mesa assembles itself for us. Your mesa, your objects of power will come to you by the healing of your own wounds. When Munay (love) becomes the principle in our life, Nature will bring you gifts of power whether you are in nature, or in the city, it makes no difference. The Universe will respond to you actively and directly whether you are in the mountains or the jungle.

Often the question about the elements and their relationship to the directions on the mesa is asked when discussing the placing of power objects or stones on the mesa. While everyone working with energy needs to understand elements, to be able to balance them in a situation or in a person they are working with, we do not need to be concerned with how they are laid out on an Andean mesa. The shape of the stones or what they represent to us is what is important when placing power objects on a mesa, not their aspects as elements. They are placed depending on the directional aspect or archetype they represent, or the wounds they heal, not by what element they represent.

An altar where you use incenses, candles, and place objects representing the elements in specific areas are used in many spiritual or magical traditions. These are usually home or church altars and are very important for our spiritual growth, but a church or home altar is not the same thing as a personal mesa. A mesa is a power bundle that connects the Shaman to power through objects given to them by the Universe. Many people have several altars; one to use for the Fire ceremony, one that is stationary in the home, one that honors the ancestors, and of course their mesa that holds and protects their medicine or personal power.

Anytime you are doing ceremony, you may use and honor the elements by placing objects that represent them in whatever area you believe they belong. It is very appropriate and adds power to incorporate them into the ceremony, or onto your altars.

Going to the Mesa!

Mesa also means mountain, or table top. Going to the mesa
would be to go to the Mountain, to the Source, using our tools
to receive answers or assistance in knowing what to do.

Using the Mesa, either mentally, or actually physically using your Pi
stone to travel around the directions, meditating and contemplating on
a situation you would like more information on is a very powerful and
helpful Divination tool. Divination is the art of using 'tools' to find an
answer within the self. Often, we go to others to have that done. We
have a card reading, a rune reading, see a pastor, or go to a counselor.
This is all valid for divining answers, but in truth, especially for someone
with Shamanic training, we can find answers ourselves. The mesa drawn
below has questions that might be asked in a specific direction. They
are just suggestions to help stimulate you to receiving a revelation from
the Universe. Use your intuition, adding to or shifting the suggested
questions. Have fun, be open, and let the Divine Source, or your Power
Animals assist you! I have found it really doesn't matter where you start,
just start asking questions and contemplating! If you can't get an answer
from one direction at first, travel to the next! Keep circling around either
clockwise or counter-clockwise until you do get answers!

North
"What needs to be born or reborn?"
"What technique could shift this situation?"
"How do my ancestors fit into this situation?"

West
"What needs to die in this situation?"
"What needs to be different?"
"What needs to be nurtured?"

East
"What do I need to see?"
"What is a higher perspective?"
"What are my possibilities if this were shed?"

South
"What is the problem or wound?"
"What needs to be shed or healed?"
"What do I need to clear from my life?"

Example of using the Mesa for Divination

Use a Pi stone with your mesa or a cloth that could represent a mesa, and asking questions is a really powerful way to get some answers! Begin by opening sacred space, then personal space, now lay the cloth in front of you and place your Pi stone on it asking the questions you want answered. For example, I will use the question, "Why do I keep forgetting to wear shoes?" Move the Pi stone to each of the directions in turn asking questions that relate to that direction for information.

When the Pi stone is in the South you ask and contemplate, "What is the wound around shoes for me?" Sometimes the answer comes quickly, sometime you have to contemplate a while, and sometime you just go on to the next direction and come back to that one later.

Then you move the Pi stone to the West and ask, "What am I afraid of about shoes?" Or call to the Jaguar saying, "Jaguar help me stalk myself and find out my aversion to shoes."

Next you move your stone to the North and ask, "What can the Ancestors tell me about shoes? What techniques or tools could I use to assist me with my shoe aversion?" Or call to the Hummingbird saying, "Hummingbird, help me make the journey to a better understanding of shoes."

Then you move your Pi stone to the East and ask, "What is the possible benefit for me if I started wearing shoes, and stopped forgetting to put them on?" or "What would life where I remembered my shoes look like, feel like, sound like, smell like, etc...? How would I live life without an aversion to my shoes?"

Now you can go back and forth to the different directions as needed. Sometimes you may want to start in the East with the possible wonderfulness of shoes, then you may move to any direction to get information. If you moved to the North you ask how to make that journey. If you moved to the West you would ask what the fear was or how the ego controls you. In the South you would ask what the wound or stuck energy is that is keeping you in this shoeless state.

Sometimes you may get a revelation and go back to a direction for more clarity or because you had not gotten information there yet, or you want a deeper meaning of what you received. For example, you may have gotten suddenly, "I am not afraid of shoes, I was just told 'we cannot afford them' as a child!" So you go back to the South to look at the 'real' wound, maybe asking, "What is this wound of not affording shoes?" Then maybe you get a revelation, "Oh this is not my wound, this is a family wound I am connected to and told to me out of poverty consciousness!" Then you can wonder, "Where did this come from? How does it really belong to, Mother, Father, Grandparents? Why am I owning it or calling this to myself?"

Maybe it is energy stuck in your auric energy field, so you go to the North again and think....or ask...."What technique can the ancestors give me to find this stuck energy?".....Ah yes, I can do a journey....So you do a journey asking the Power Animals and guides to 'show' you where you got this stuck energy that manifests itself in you not wearing shoes......And maybe you get a past life about a poor child not wearing shoes, or something else.....You see it, so you can bless and release it. If it is intense, like unworthiness then you do the techniques you will learn in the next chapter about finding yourself at your death and releasing yourself. When you are finished and have the answers you needed, you can go back to the East and 'see' the possibility of life with lots of shoes, where you love shoes. Usually once you find 'it', the reason or wound that causes your difficulty and transmute the energy, things shift automatically. You don't really need to recreate a better life with shoes, your subconscious will do that for you.

CHAPTER 8

Triangle of Disempowerment

The whole training was about remembering where I come from.
- Fredy "Puma" Quispe Singona

Wisdom in the Shamanic tradition is about connecting to ancient knowledge which requires us to move into the level of the Hummingbird or the Soul in the North. To begin to work on a Soul level to make effective changes to our life dream we must learn to use ancient healing techniques to connect to our personal destiny. We must become Wisdom Keepers. Reading, learning, studying, attending workshops on spirituality are all important but unless you use the information or techniques, they are not effective for change. Learning and studying is not enough for healing of the self.

To become a Wisdom Keeper, one who knows and protects ancient wisdom, we must stop and look at our personal stories. We must use techniques to release our fear of death so we can then see what we need to shed. When we understand the triangle of disempowerment we can begin to live a life outside the story created by our personal wounds. It is then we can embrace Wisdom internalizing it and releasing the deepest level of our wounds, our disempowering story.

When we live within the script of our stories we create what is called a trauma bond, or a triangle of disempowerment. The leading actors in our tale or life story are always acting out of one of three roles of this trauma bond. The characters are in the form of the victim, the perpetrator, or the rescuer. In the Native American World they could be called the Indian, the Conquistador, and the Priest. What often adds to the confusion within our stories is that the role we feel cast in is often not the same as what others think we are cast in. The North American Indians were viewed as a perpetrator by the settlers yet they felt they were the victims. They felt the settlers were the perpetrators because they were stealing their land. To the Native Americans, the Priests were not saviors, they were perpetrators. Yet the Priest believed they were rescuing the Natives, saving their very souls.

In the Western culture we are often taught to believe that we must suffer to be a good person, that the victim role is honorable. We often shift back and forth from victim to rescuer because we define perpetrators as evil. Oddly, when we are trying to rescue our children or friends they believe they are being victimized and we are the perpetrator, yet we are sure we are rescuing them from difficulty! When we war with or fight to help other cultures, we often do so to save them from themselves or their evil governments. We are sure we are rescuing them, yet they usually feel perpetrated or victimized. The lines between the rescuer and the perpetrator get blurred so that eventually people just choose to continue to be victims to whatever situation comes their way to avoid the other two choices. They do not wish to die on a cross, nor do they want to be cruel to others, so they allow themselves to be victims to poverty, to remaining in relationships where they are not free to grow, or to unhappiness, or difficulty.

We are all the lead players in our life story and often switch characters as our story unfolds. We often rotate through the three roles in our relationship with ourselves as well as with others. We perpetrate ourselves out of guilt or fear. We hold on to the victim role because of our family programming while at the same time trying to rescue ourselves by searching out the newest self-help technique or relationship book.

Our life stories are so powerful and convincing that they get internalized and lodge in our muscle tissue as cellular memories. Whatever the image you have of yourself in your story, you will embody it, and people will respond to you in that way. We continue to cling to our role because we derive some benefit from it on some level, even when it causes us suffering. Usually the main payoff is that our ego sees itself as a star if we remain part of the drama. Another benefit of clinging to our stories is that they give us a false sense of security and purpose, a reason or logic to our perceived reality.

We can never heal ourselves by staying within our story. We must shed our belief in our role like the snake sheds its skin. When we shed our negative, unoriginal stories we are free to shift to appreciate what we gain from our experiences. In any situation, healing is most likely to occur when a person is able to break out of character, step out of the story and stop judging it as right or wrong. When we realize that what we call right or wrong are just assumptions based on what society told us, we can stop judging our story and accept it as it is. We can then embrace the facts but reject the negative interpretations. We are then free to discard the old story where we play one of the three disempowered roles. Then we can script a new story that includes what we learned, celebrating our new understanding or compassion. This will change our dream and release us from suffering because we will be free from the limitations created by the part we cast ourselves in.

We can change our stories, step out of our roles and in doing so heal and change our lives, but to do this we must first begin by identifying the roles we have cast ourselves in. This is difficult and takes releasing the denial we may have lived with for years. It will help to take the position of the observer looking at our story in relation to the four directions on the mesa. In the South we shed our roles by understanding that it was through our wounds that we created them. In the West we release our fear of change and what caused us to create them in the first place. In the North we observe and associate with our soul instead of the ego, changing the trauma story into a journey statement, embracing the lessons we learned in our situation. Then in the East we consciously choose to rewrite our script changing our dream.

Starting at the South, begin by realizing that everyone sees things from a different perspective. Look at your story realizing that the role you place yourself in may not be the role others see you in. We know that no two people can be in the same place and report it the same. As an example, consider the story of the blind Hindu Holy men who sat around an elephant, each trying to describe it to the others. The one that felt the tail stated the elephant was like a rope, the one that touched the trunk said an elephant was like a hose. The holy man that held the ear claimed an elephant was like a leaf, and the one that felt his leg claimed an elephant was like a large tree trunk. They were all wrong, yet they were all right. When we realize this, we begin to see and understand that in truth none of our stories are completely true. They are just scripts we have created that keep us stuck in the past.

The South teaches us to shed what no longer serves us, which includes our family roles or cultural myths. When you reflect in the South you look to see what needs to be shed. You ask the questions, "What is my role in this story? How is it defined by me, and how is it defined by others? What needs to be shed for me to step out of this trauma bond?"

Throughout the next few days, be in the South asking to recognize the three roles, seeing how they play out in your interactions with others. Spend time observing others interactions as well as defining the roles they are playing. Then begin to observe the way the two interplay. This is the first step to becoming an observer, the first step to freedom. Once we 'see' what we are doing, how we have chosen to interact in various situations, we can choose not to do it anymore. We can choose to end the way we encounter, or interact with others and ourselves.

An important step in freeing yourself from the triangle of disempowerment is to allow others their choices. Instead of pointing out to them that they have cast you in a particular role, just step out of the triangle and choose to act differently, or walk away. This work on awareness is about you and your personal healing, not about your helping others now. Realize the role they have cast you in comes from their dream, their imprisonment within the trauma bond, and don't take it personally. Allowing is the main word when dealing with others. We can allow them their dream and still change our dream. Also, to stop perpetrating yourself includes not judging yourself when you forget about the various roles. When you find you have cast yourself in one of the three roles again and are acting accordingly, just stop to observe it, step out, and choose again.

Now for more understanding we continue around the mesa looking at the West. Here we discover the power of fearlessness. When we focus on what we dread, we give power to it. Fear cannot be shed by understanding why we are afraid just as hunger cannot be stopped by understanding why we are starving. We must go beyond the understanding of the origins of our fears to release them. We will learn to let go of our suffering by first observing the story we have wrapped around the facts

We have been told that all our fears are really extensions of our fear of death. Our fears of losing our job, being rejected, not being safe, or not having enough money are all just the fear of death disguised, but it goes further. It is really our ego's fear of annihilation that we hold in our luminous energy field over many incarnations that is our greatest unrecognized fear. We have experienced birth and death many times. Yes we are concerned it will be painful and we will suffer emotional loss, but what we fear most is the annihilation of our ego. The ego is terrified of being absorbed back into something larger than itself. This fear is greater than the fear of physical death. Our ego presents us with the fear of death, and our psyche makes us believe there are only three roles we can create when relating to others and ourselves. This keeps us distracted from the true fear of the annihilation of our ego when it is absorbed back in to the light. When we are identifying with the ego, we are afraid, but when we identify with our soul, our fear dissolves. The ego sees life as separation, but the soul sees a connectedness to all that is. It sees Unity.

87

We can release our fear of death in the West first by understanding death is not a terminal experience, then by having closure. Death ceases to be a terminal experience when we have closure. The fear is gone. But how do we come to this level of closure to release our fear of death? We do that through Shamanic journey, finding closure in the lives where we embodied one of the three main trauma bond roles as our main life role. Although in all our lives we rotate through the three roles, there are lives, including possibly this one, where we have chosen one of these roles as our main theme.

To clear our past, we journey to the three main lifetimes: where you were the most victimized, the best rescuer, and the worse perpetrator, finding closure at our death. This will free us from repeating these roles unconsciously. We do not need to heal all the lives where we suffered, were perpetrators, or rescuers. If we find the main ones through journey and have closure in them, all the other past lives or possible future lives where we embodied those roles will be healed. To journey to our past or future lives where we truly embodied one of these roles throughout that life finding closure at our death will release us from the triangle of disempowerment. Closure is an important aspect in all healing. You must face the pain, the emotion, the situation honestly, without denial. Only then can you let it dissipate and be free from it. This is as true in everyday interactions of life as it is in the soul's journey throughout lifetimes

We come to closure with these lives by healing the last moments of that existence, by forgiving ourselves at our deaths. Assuring ourselves that all is forgiven, that we are done with being the victim, that we were the best rescuer ever, a good and faithful servant, or that we are forgiven for the perpetration we did to ourselves and others. This will bring us closure that will change how we react in this life. It releases us from life times of denial. We look at and admit who and what we were without judgment and they will release us. Consider situations in this life, how if not acknowledged, they continue to bother you. You may have a cordial relationship with an ex-lover or family member, but often there are situations that still bother or color your reality even if you are in denial about them. We must speak our truth! That we felt wronged, or that we did wrong before we can let situations dissipate and be done with their lesson!

The past lives to look at for closure are: the one in which we suffered the most, the one in which we had the greatest power and knowledge but abused it, and the one in which we had the greatest power and knowledge and used it to serve others. You can journey to these lives and tell your former selves all is forgiven, allowing your Spirit to return home in peace. In our journey, we take the role of an Angel that will reach back into the past, healing our self with observation and closure. Then, when you have cleared the lingering deaths of these three former lifetimes, you will be free to move on to the next direction, create a healed and empowered course for the next leg of your journey here on Earth. Their unconscious programming will no longer have a hold on you.

After dealing with this fear of death or annihilation we realize that real death is sleepwalking through life. We will come to understand that existing without really living is when we are lost to our destiny.

Closure with our former roles moves us to the Soul level or the North. In the North of the mesa, associating with the soul instead of the ego, we are free to connect to the ancient teachings. We then embrace the lessons the situation of our past story taught us. Our original story about an absent father becomes a new, more positive one of a child that learned the value of independence. We go from being a neglected child to one who learned independence. This new script, or what is often called a journey statement, allows us to step out of the frozen roles we had been cast in. This journey statement is done in the Soul level or North.

Yet, we must be cautious when entering the Soul level, so often the rescuer resides there. The compassion that is opened in our hearts on the Soul level often drives us to be rescuers. Once we study or know ancient teachings of wholeness we naturally want to share them and help others. What needs to be opened to our awareness is that everyone is choosing, on some level, to experience what they are creating in their personal dream. We have to hold to that truth. We need to be available for assistance when asked, but we cannot rush in blindly denying others the experiences they have chosen for themselves. To be free from the perpetrator role completely, we cannot judge ourselves or others for the experiences we programmed ourselves for before we entered into this life manifestation. We must become observers and release our judgment of situations.

As an observer, the Soul sees a connectedness to 'all that is'. In the North we understand nothing ever just happens to us and no one ever does anything to us that we have not agreed to. We understand that we have and can choose our roles and write our scripts, that we are the creator of each event and incident in our life. It is in the realization that we as Soul are connected to all that is that we realize we have the power to create whatever life or dream we want. We now know we are the creator of each event and incident in our lives.

Observation and allowing are important keys to the Soul level. They give us the compassion to shift our understanding that the current dream was created through the lens of personal wounds. Observing allows us to step out of the triangle of disempowerment, holding the understanding that we are in fact, spiritual beings having a human experience. We then see that each interaction with others is truly an interaction with ourselves. We realize each interaction is a projection of both our shadow and light, knowing now that we can choose differently if we want to. Remember it is important to change our disempowering story into a journey statement, what we learned or what was given to us on our journey.

In the East we move into the level of the Eagle or Condor becoming the Sage that dreams the world into being, that sees life from a higher perspective. We then can sit in meditation envisioning a world we would like our children to inherit. We can envision a dream we want to participate in. It is here, as the observer, that we come to the knowing that life just mirrors our own beliefs. If we are unhappy with our choices, after identifying them and accepting that they were created by our belief, we can choose to change our belief which will recreate our life dream. If your beliefs don't serve you, change your beliefs. Remember, effectiveness is the measure of truth. Are your choices and beliefs giving you the effectiveness you want? If not, change them.

Here in the East we first see what needs to find closure in our lives. We review our trip around the mesa, looking at our stories and ask, "What needs closure in this situation? In my life? What beliefs need to be shed? What does this story tell about soul growth or what is the soul level information to be taken from this story? What beliefs have held me to this particular dream or story?" After receiving information, and you will in meditation or through journey, move into writing a new story, or dreaming a new dream. Make sure you have first changed the old disempowering story into a journey statement, reflecting on the positive lessons learned from it. This allows choice. It allows us to step out of the triangle of disempowerment. Becoming an observer in this way frees us.

Now we are ready to consciously rewrite our script, dreaming our destiny of choice into being. This rewriting of our scripts begins by asking ourselves, "Who am I if I am not my pain, or my disease, or my problems?" We then look at each encounter with others or the disempowering energy of our story seeing the role we are playing without judgment. Remember others may not see your role the same way. Knowing that gives us the understanding that each role within the triangle of disempowerment is subjective. We then ask ourselves, "What would we like our life or dream to look like since we now know all things are possible? What would our choices be?" And most importantly, we contemplate the possibilities we could have in this new dream. Sitting in meditation, we envision the life or dream we want, without limitations then begin to embody it through imagery; what it would look like, feel like, sound like or smell like.

When we master this 'art of dreaming with our eyes open' at the Eagle level, we stop going through life unconsciously. We stop living the collective nightmare and become authors of our own life no longer continuing to live our stories as the victim, rescuer or perpetrator. We can choose to be free from the limitations of our stories instead of clinging to them in order to give ourselves a false sense of security. At this level we can also learn to dream a world of grace and beauty into being even when awake.

In summary, in the South at the Serpent level death is on a physical plane. Death means the heart stops and your brain waves cease. At the Jaguar level of the mind in the West, death causes us to have fear concerning the loss of the sense of self, that this may be the only time around as 'us'. This great fear is overcome with journey and finding closure with our past lives. At the level of the soul or Hummingbird in the North, we see death as the beginning of a journey to another lifetime, family, or body. We change our disempowering story to a journey statement of power, a statement that reflects what we have learned so we can let it go, be free from it! We change our perspective of the story, which releases its hold on us. Here we realize we are a spiritual being born to experience the physical world and in doing so learn to love completely. In the East, at the level of Spirit or the Eagle we have the realization we are a being of conscious energy that dwells outside of time choosing our experiences, and creating our own dream. We come to realize that we never truly die but continue through infinity, that we are energy that is never destroyed or created. We recognize that we are infinite and that death is simply a change of skin, a new adventure which causes us to realize we can choose our part in our play, opening ourselves to the ability to choose what we want and create our reality or dream. Through journey, affirmation, calling on our guides or Power Animals, we can sit in meditation choosing our beliefs, creating a new dream for ourselves. We embody this new dream by seeing, feeling, hearing the new dream. We use our senses.

We rewrite the script by choosing what we want to experience, then sit and dream it into being with the use of imagery. Then you let it go! We release it to allow the Universe to make it reality for us. Our job is to determine what we want, the Universe will provide how it comes into manifestation. Manifestation comes about when we choose clearly what we want, affirm our desire is already fulfilled in the spirit, visualize our fulfillment, then release the idea or dream to let the Universe do the work. Yes, act on any ideas that come to you, take action of sorts, but allow the work to be done for you, accept it as if it has already happened. And one last most important comment, spend time in meditation and journey. Daily, quietly sit with thoughts of infinity, of possibility. The world is in reality limitless, full of all possibility but you must give yourself permission to be successful, be happy, be confident, and be positive. It is in a meditative state you program and clear the subconscious mind. It is through journey that you clear and find what needs closure so you can shift. Remember, the world is what you decide it is. There are no limits, energy flows where attention goes, and now is the moment of power. Remember also, to love is to be happy with, and all power comes from within.

CHAPTER 9

Working with Energy

We each have the ability to release and draw energy – we all do it.
- Llyn Roberts & Robert Levy

P ower in the Andean Shamanic tradition is often referred to as the ability to 'push the Kawsay' (cows-eye), to have a conscious interchange with the Kawsay Pacha or cosmos of living energy. This refers to the ability to work with energy, clearing and reordering it. It is about having a relationship of reciprocity, or Ayni with the cosmos. The Universe or Kawsay Pacha is not a complex world, it is quite simple. It is composed of an animating energy much like a spectrum similar to light and color that moves from ordered energy to disordered energy. The consciousness of our energy world dawns at our birth and intensifies through our life aligning and connecting us with the energies of the physical and Spirit realms. Our job as Shaman is to keep this energy ordered, and cleared.

The Kawsay Pacha or the Cosmos is made of living energy that intensifies throughout life and can align and connect us with the elements and the energies of both the physical and Spirit realms. The most light, ordered energy is called Sami (sahm-ee) in this tradition. It is energy in its natural fundamental unspoiled state and is the most compatible with our own original state. Filled with this ordered energy, we are empowered, energetic and healthy. Sami (sahm-ee) imparts power to natural objects and the places where it accumulates. Our natural state is to be filled with this refined, ordered, light energy and we feel enlivened when we come into contact with Sami in a sacred site or natural power place.

In contrast Hucha (who-cha) is heavy, disordered, dense energy less compatible with the human energy field. It also accumulates in many places which affects us when we come into contact with it. When filled with it we are unhappy, sick, and depressed. Hucha or disorganized energy is created by negative human emotions.

Life in the material world, where our thoughts and actions are driven by human emotions, disturbs Sami energy causing it to become disordered and heavy, to become Hucha. Humans are the only beings that create Hucha. It manifests because we do not live in perfect Ayni or reciprocity with the cosmos or with each other. At our current level of consciousness humans cannot seem to exist on Pachamama (Mother Earth) without upsetting the harmony of the environment making Hucha impossible to avoid. They cannot stop hurting each other, the environment, or themselves. Any space humans occupy be it congested city streets or fields of flowers has Hucha.

Hucha is accumulated through emotional interactions with other and keeps us in energetic disorder so that we do not function optimally. It prevents us from engaging with the Kawsay Pacha or Cosmos as fully as we can. The work of the Shaman is to monitor energy exchanges making Sami the dominant energy in the flow of exchange coming from you and to you in the Kawsay Pacha. Our task as 'light workers' or as the Andeans call 'Children of the Sun' is to be aware of the energy in our bodies and environments so we can transform Hucha back into Sami, so we live with a greater sense of wellbeing. The more Sami or light energy we increase in our lives, and the more Hucha we cleanse from our energy systems, the more we move toward our natural state and raise our level of consciousness.

Hucha is not in itself negative or bad, there is no moral judgment in this tradition. It is just disorder in our energy field. What we believe or judge as bad about misaligned dense energy are the symptoms of the accumulation of it. Fear or pain, hurtful behaviors, poor self-image and the like are symptoms of being in contact with Hucha energy. The more misaligned energy we acquire the worse we feel because it becomes too heavy for our energy field. Heaviness is relative, what is too heavy for one person may not be too heavy for someone else. This makes the perception of Hucha energy relative to the condition of the Shaman's poq'po (pok-po) or energy body and the energetic power they have at their disposal. This is an important concept because it helps us stop judging any energy as evil, bad, or negative, but puts the responsibility of the quality of energy interchanges squarely on how well we can push the Kawsay, or move and clear energy.

When we shift our perspective away from judgment, suddenly there is nothing to protect ourselves from. Now instead of good or bad energy we simply recognize energy as incompatible with our own then act to transform it. Even if the Hucha feels too heavy for you to handle at the time, it presents no danger to you. There is no need to close off the energy body in an attempt to be protected from negative situations. Let energy be like a stone you are trying to move in a garden, if it is too heavy for you to lift, just let it be, do not fight it or try to move it until you become stronger or get assistance. There is no need to judge it or fear it, because the stone (misaligned energy) in itself cannot hurt you.

Most energy that we perceive as evil is energy upon which we have projected our own fears. And sometimes what appears to us as a dark energy is often a trickster or nature spirit that is challenging or testing us to help us move through our psychological or spiritual blocks. They are really here in disguise to help empower us. We need to act reasonably with the energies we perceive as dark. Our initial reaction of wanting to protect ourselves or fight 'evil' actually makes it stronger because it reinforces the duality of our projection. Energies we perceive as evil cannot do anything to us that we do not consciously or unconsciously agree to. This is where the accumulation of personal power comes into play. Personal power is not about domination but about the command of your personal energy. A more productive response is to open a dialogue with an energy or entity that generates fear within us creating the opportunity for our fear to fall away so we can deal with the energy at a less emotional level in a more energetically mature way.

Within this sacred tradition, energy has no moral category, but how one pushes the Kawsay can potentially harm you or others. A Shaman and a Sorcerer both work with energy but they work with different intents according to their moral systems. Most Paqos (pah-ko) or Shaman would admit that you can do harm by pushing the Kawsay Pacha for your own selfish or devious ends.

Our task as 'light workers' or as the Andeans call 'Children of the Sun' is to be aware of the energy in our bodies and environments so we can transform Hucha back into Sami living with a greater sense of wellbeing. When we cleanse heavy energy configurations we feed it back to Pachamama who reorders the energy into Sami. The more Sami or light energy we increase in our lives, and the more Hucha we cleanse from our energy systems, the more we move toward our natural state and raise our level of consciousness.

The capacity to cleanse energy is connected to our understanding and our consciousness of Ayni, to the understanding that we have a ceaseless energetic interchange with others and with the natural world. No matter what technique you use to clear energy, you always give or feed the Hucha to Pachamama. She loves Hucha, or disorganized energy. It empowers her. It is food to her and in return for her energetic meal she returns Sami or refined energy to the person doing the cleansing. The Earth needs this living energy and as we release Hucha to her empowering her we are empowering ourselves. Energy is neither created nor destroyed, it just gets disorganized making it heavy, or is reorganized making it lighter.

Before doing any energy work, including clearing, always ground yourself. There are many ways to do this, smudging, drumming, opening sacred space, for example. The fastest, easiest way is to imagine that your feet go deep into the ground and roots grow out of your feet and into the earth. When you are finished clearing, or doing energy work, you draw the roots back out of the ground and into your feet.

Clearing Energy – Saminchukuy (sah-min-chas-ka)

Here is a powerful release technique. Sit in a meditative state and ground yourself to begin. When you are ready, visualize any Hucha in your auric energy field or body being drawn into the second root chakra like it was a magnet and the Hucha was iron fillings. Draw this misaligned energy into the second and first charkra areas. Next, image a stopper like one in an old bathtub in the root chakra (where the body meets the legs) and visualize pulling out this stopper. The Hucha accumulated in these lower chakras and what is still being drawn into the lower chakras flows out the first chakra, down the legs and into the Earth. As this release is occurring, simultaneously draw in Sami energy through the crown chakra on top of your head. Use a visualization of screwing open the top of the head seeing a golden ball of light beam Sami into the crown chakra. The Sami energy coming into the crown chakra goes down through the body flushing the Hucha you have drawn in from the body and aura out the first chakra, down the legs, and into the Earth. When you feel that you have cleared your Hucha, first stop the imaginary magnet from drawing in Hucha then put the stopper back into your first charkra. Now allow the body begin to fill with Sami energy. Keep filling the body with the golden light or Sami energy until you feel it overflow out the top of your head surrounding your entire body and filling the aura. When you feel complete, screw the crown chakra closed and allow the golden ball of light to dissipate or go into your heart.

Locating your Qosqo (Kos-ko)

Although there are several ways to clear energy, using the qosqo is the main way of the Peruvian Shaman. Qosqo is a Quechua word meaning stomach or navel. It is our spiritual stomach and in this tradition it is considered the primary energy center. It is located at the area around our navel, or the second chakra. To perceive energies or intentionally interchange energy with the cosmos or another person, it helps to learn to use this center, sensitizing yourself on how it operates. This brings it under your conscious control.

Sit in a meditative state for a few moments and ground yourself. Place your hands over your belly, around your navel area, a few inches above the skin or clothing at the second chakra. Bring your awareness to the space between your hand and your navel feeling the warmth that is generated by your body. Move your hands around slowly just a few inches side to side making a circle in an attempt to feel this opening. After a few moments you should be able to distinguish a more or less circular area of energy, a concentrated warmth, tingling sensation, or a sticky pulling feeling. However you perceive it, when you do, notice its edges and boundaries. This area is your qosqo or the buckle of the energy belt of your poq'po (energy body) that surrounds the lower midsection of your body. The eye or buckle of this belt is usually situated slightly below the navel though it may have shifted to one side or the other. Sense the density of energy in this area to locate this energy center in your belt of power. Let your intuition guide you as you attempt to feel it.

Once you have sensed the approximate parameters of your spiritual stomach or energy center, begin to open your hands farther away from your skin or clothing, a little at a time. Try to sense the warmth extending and opening outward. You are extending your poq'po (energy body) and your qosqo is opening, creating a larger energy center. Practice sensing and pulling it outward until your arms are fully extended both out and open. It is like you are reaching and opening your arms to hug a short child. At this point your qosqo is considered wide open. After feeling it open, bring your hands back in toward the body to close the belt. Practice this technique, moving your hands outward from your body and then back to the body again, pulling your energy out and open, contracting your energy body and closing this energy center. The qosqo can be visualized as a camera lens or an eye whose pupil dilates as it lets in more light then contracts to let in less. When you have consistent control of extending and drawing back in the energy center of your spiritual stomach at the belt of power, opening and closing the eye of this energy with your hand, switch to using only your mind and intention to open and close this center. Always take a moment to clear your energy with the release technique after working with your spiritual stomach, when practicing or when doing other exercises learning to connect and feel energy. This will help to keep you clear.

Harmonizing with a Nature Energy

A good way to begin to work with and understand the spiritual stomach is to sit in meditation with an elemental object in front of you practicing opening your qosqo and feeling the energy of the object. Start with a candle and feel fire. Then a bowl of water, a crystal, a plant, or other objects that are related to the elements. Remember to ground yourself before you work with the elements and to clear yourself afterwards, more as a way of getting yourself into the habit than anything else. It is a good idea to journal afterwards so you can remember your experience.

After you feel comfortable with that, choose an object in nature that is an entity unto itself, a tree, a hill, a rock formation. Sit about three feet away from it. For nature entities like sand, rain or wind, you may immerse yourself in them. Settle yourself for a few minutes using grounding and using whatever relaxation technique is most comfortable and effective for you. Attune to your energy body and open your qosqo. As you make energetic contact with the natural object be alert to subtle changes of temperature or density in your qosqo area, and to colors and texture that may appear in your inner vision. Do not analyze any of these sensations or visions, just experience them and let them go. If at any time you feel uncomfortable, pull your poq'po in closer to your physical body, closing your qosqo until it is just a small opening and end the exercise.

Always clear yourself with the release technique, feeding the energy down into Mother Earth after working with energy. If you feel uncomfortable in any way after an exercise of connecting to energy, lay down on the ground, belly to belly with the Mother, and release all your Hucha out through your poq'po. As you release Hucha, pull refined Sami energy in through your head or Crown chakra.

Harmonizing Shamanic Practices

The periods of sunrise and sunset are the hours of power, the transitional time when the energy flows most freely. The best place to start sensitizing yourself to the Kawsay Pacha (Universe) is by working with your energy body at sunrise and sunset. Working with the Moon, the Sun's counterpart is also a powerful way to sensitize yourself to energy. Practice harmonizing with the Sun or the Moon for at least a month, then once every season.

Harmonizing with the Setting Sun

Make sure you are settled comfortably out of doors at least ten minutes before sunset. Dress comfortably according to the season. Choose a place free of distractions and away from large bodies of water as they are particularly powerful nature energies and may pull your awareness from the sunset. Let the sunset be the focus of your environment. Settle yourself by meditating for a few minutes focusing your awareness on your breath and try to empty your mind of every day concerns. When you are relaxed, attune yourself to your poq'po and bring your attention to your qosqo, opening the center a little at a time, focusing your inner awareness on the Sun. If you do not yet have intentional control of your qosqo, use your hands to draw it outward and fully open. Keeping your eyes closed, feel the Sun and its movement with your energy body. Try to sense the Sun's dimming, it's sinking. Reach out with your energetic perception to 'see' the effect of the Sun's changing light on the sky and landscape. Continue gently until you feel that the Sun has gone down. Attune yourself to what a sunset feels like physically but also awaken all your other senses. What does the sunset look like through closed eyes? What does it taste like? Smell like? Notice these sensory impressions then release them and attune yourself to the energetic feeling you sense through your qosqo. After a month of sensing sunsets, you should be aware of the myriad nuances of the movement of energy of a setting Sun.

Harmonizing with the Rising Sun

Repeat the exercise above, for one month during sunrise. How does the energetic 'feel' of the environment change as the Sun rises and infuses your world with light and heat? How does a rising Sun feel energetically different from a setting Sun? Is there a different 'taste' to the energy?

Harmonizing with the Moon

Choose a time of night when the moon is high in the sky, and over two consecutive months go outside at the same time of the evening and repeat the technique of harmonizing only this time with the Moon. Be sure to give yourself at least twenty minutes and keep your eyes closed as you sense the Moon. Attune to your poq'po, open your qosqo, and see if you can sense the changing conditions of the Moon. When does a cloud cross in front of it? Did you feel a shooting star? During the course of a month, how does the Moon's energy change with its phases? How is the Moon's energy different from the Sun's? Can you taste the difference between the masculine nature energy (Sun) and the feminine nature energy (Moon)?

Harmonizing with the Stars

Repeat the same sensing exercise for one month but instead of focusing on the Moon, focus on the Stars. You may choose one Star on which to focus your energy attention on or simply give yourself over to the entire field of Stars. Although energetically it does not matter if you can physically see the Stars or not, it is preferable that they be visible if for no other reason than their beauty which inspires us to practice!

Understanding Transformation and Journeying between two Elements

This is a technique to help learn to control both your 'seeing' and your energy body. It works with the breath. When we intentionally place our consciousness between different elements we are able to experience something of their magical or spiritual nature. We can use their ability to reach out to each other to change and be changed, to transform and be transformed. When we focus our minds and energy between the wave and the beach, the fire and the log, the root and the soil, the bud and the stem, the drop of rain and the leaf, the blanket of new snow and the crust of old snow we can experience the transformations occurring between these elements. We begin to be aware of a type of transformation that occurs intentionally and purposefully between the elements and ourselves. We come to know the Spirits of these elements in the ways they know themselves. We begin to think like a river, see like a mountain, feel like a tree. We understand the intelligent nature of nonhuman beings in ways that we cannot fathom from the perspective of ordinary awareness. We then realize our kinship with the natural elements and discover that there is no separation between us and them on the spiritual level.

Exercise: Begin by being aware of the place between our breaths. Here we become aware of the still point places in our breathing. Slow your breathing down, take deeper, more complete breaths and notice the points at the top and bottom of each breath where there is a slight pause. These are the points where the inhale turns into an exhale and where an exhale becomes the next inhale. Both are places of transformation. As you breathe, do not hold your breath or pause at these points, or you will turn them into fixed places and they will lose their insubstantial quality of being 'neither this, nor that.' So allow each inhale to flow naturally into the exhale, and vice versa. Without pausing, notice what it feels like when you become conscious of the spaces, as you move gently through and beyond them. Try to experience them as places outside of time and space, as conditions that are composed of neither the act of inhaling nor the act of exhaling. After you are comfortable with this begin to observe the act of pausing. Take at least ten breaths to experience this elusive quality and then contemplate or write in a journal trying to describe the experience.

The second stage of this practice is to send your consciousness away from your own field of energy to mingle with the consciousness of two elements in front of you, to a place where they are actively engaged with each other. Find two elements in nature, or you may place a rock in a bowl of water or light a candle to work with. Before you begin the exercise decide where you wish to send your Spirit to. That way you will not have to interrupt your practice by making a decision. Let's say you have chosen the place between the rock and the water. After you have observed about ten breaths as described above, send your attention, consciousness or Spirit out to the place where the rock and the water meet, those spaces between the atoms, where their energy blends, where their auras meet, where their Spirits are engaged in the dance of life. Hold your consciousness between the rock and the water for as long as you can. When you are ready, withdraw it into yourself again. Go back to focus on your breathing again, before coming back. Journaling is very helpful after this exercise to remember the experience.

CHAPTER 10

Imagery, Blessing and Shamanic Poetry

"The Mind is everything. What you think, you become."
– Buddha

The way to recreate our dream is the way we have created the dream we live in now, through imagery. We create our reality from the images we hold in our mind. The word images in this context include feelings, sounds, tastes, smells, and memories. Most of what we have created both in the larger social dream and in our personal dream comes from the images we have been given by society filtered through our wounds. Once we understand the truth of how we have been programmed by images, we can actively choose to monitor them being more selective of what we put into the mind.

We change the world by who we become, by our presence in the world. This includes learning how to transmute negative states of consciousness that arise throughout the day. Clearing our Hucha and our environment is important, but the next step is to shift the images held in mind, to reprogram the mind. Our inner world creates the outer world we live in so it is important that we become dreamers that hold the vision of the world we want, not what we don't want. We must work to shift from being dreamers that dream by default into creators of what we want. The true Shaman and mystics are not limited by the collective beliefs of what is possible, but are open to create from the realm of all possibility. The Shaman becomes the rain to make it rain, becomes prosperity to shift into becoming prosperous, or is healed by holding the images of wholeness. How is this done? Through the imagery of the mind!

All people use their minds to create but most do this unconsciously. You can look at their life and environment and know what they are thinking. The Shaman 'sees' the current dream, acknowledges the imagery, then consciously changes the dream by actively shifting and recreating new images in their mind.

It is difficult for most people to change their dream or reality because when you ask them what they want, they either don't know, or don't know how to describe what they want. When they finally do know what they want and try to explain it, they are ambiguous, often unable to expand on the description. Few people have a way to describe life or situations that don't include violence, anger, rejection, competition, loss or lack. They have to take time to stop, reword or rethink their language if they do wish to think or speak from a place of beauty instead. With this understanding, we realize why it is important for the Shaman to learn to create images of Beauty in the mind.

A Shaman uses art and poetry to learn to see the world of beauty and describe it in a way that connects them to the Divine Source. Practicing Shamanic poetry is one way to learn to 'speak' differently. It programs the mind giving the ability to spontaneously bring forth positive language helping to create a dream or life of beauty by teaching us to observe and reflect on the beauty of the world. It then becomes easier to create beauty in our lives and personal dreams. It also gives a way to dialogue with the Divine other than supplication, pleading or bargaining with an outside source.

Our old ways of communicating with Source reinforces that God is outside of us and we need to beg and ask for assistance. The Shamanic way, based on poetry, acknowledges that Source is all around and within us. Practicing Shamanic poetry creates images of beauty in our minds that we can draw from when creating our own dreams. I reinforce that we are all filled with that one power and have the right and privilege of using it for creating better lives for ourselves and our world right here and now.

Shamanic poetry uses three important tools of Shamanism: seeing, gratitude, and blessing. Seeing allows us to see our projections or the projections of others. We use Shamanic journey or guided meditation to see our guides, to see our wounds and by seeing them, transmute them. It also refers to the knowing that all is Divine Source. All is God.

Gratitude opens the heart so you have the gateway to journey and travel. Situations remain similar in form until we appreciate them. You have created what you have and what you are. You must first be grateful for the lessons you have brought yourself, be grateful for where you are, then you can move on to something else, or something better. It is incredibly difficult, almost impossible to shift, change or increase something in your life until you are grateful for what you have first.

Blessing is the concept of manifesting and healing through the spoken word of kindness and love. It is considered a form of Ayni, or reciprocity. What we bless with our creative acts, thoughts, and words blesses us in return. Whatever we give out, we get back. So bless whatever you see: people, places or situations and the blessing will not only help them, it will help you.

Words spoken aloud create change and healing, and what you give out to others in love and kindness return to you. Words are more effective if spoken aloud but blessings can be given to people and situations in your meditation, silently as they pass by or when a person or situation comes through your mind. The prayers that the Shaman uses for healing or in ceremony are also known as blessings. The job of the Shaman includes blessing everything! "The Lord's blessing is our greatest wealth; all our work adds nothing to it." (Proverbs 10:22).

It is also important to ask for blessings for ourselves as well as others. "Ask and you shall receive" (Mathew 7:7) is a Karmic law.

Before my understanding of the Beauty Way, like the majority of humanity, I believed that an outside source must 'do' or 'advocate' for us. Now I know that the Divine is within us, so we are the ones that must do the advocating for ourselves and our clients.

There are many powerful prayers from many different sources that can be transformed to demonstrate the three Shamanic tools of gratitude, seeing and blessing. Using favorite prayers as templates then shifting them, the Shaman of the Beauty Way can create powerful blessing prayers. Here is an example of how to do that using a very powerful prayer from the Bible, called the prayer of Jabez. (1 Chronicles 4:10).

'And Jabez called on the God of Israel saying, "Oh, that You will bless me indeed, and enlarge my territory, that Your hand would be with me, and that You would keep me from evil, that I may not cause pain."' So God granted him what he requested.

Here is how this prayer could read transformed in the Shaman's way that uses gratitude, seeing and blessing. "Thank you Divine Source, you have blessed me indeed, and I see everything around me continues to be enlarged and expanded! I am grateful for your continued blessings! I see that you are within me and all things and that this awareness and knowing has protected me! Let me be a blessing to all, that I may create beauty and joy!"

Below are some basic templates to use and work with to learn Shamanic poetry, so that you can learn to think and speak from the Beauty Way.

Exercise: Spend time writing or speaking poetry using these forms as a template. Do not vary from the format! Insert different words or ideas in the blanks for practice, but use the same wording format. Just look around and put anything in the blank. You will notice it changes everything!

You are the _____of my joy (or love).
Example: You are the <u>neighbor</u> of my <u>love</u>.
Example: You are the <u>cow</u> of my <u>joy</u>.
Example: You are the <u>mountain</u> of my <u>joy</u>.
Example: You are the <u>husband</u> of my <u>love</u>.

Beautiful the _____ Beautiful too the _____
Example: Beautiful the <u>rising sun</u>, beautiful too the <u>shadow it casts</u>.
Example: Beautiful the <u>morning dew</u>, beautiful too the <u>grass where it lies</u>.
Example: Beautiful the <u>clouds</u>, beautiful too the <u>blue sky</u>.

As the _____(something in nature)
May my_____(something in your life)

Example: As the <u>sun rises</u>,
        May my <u>soul warm with gratitude</u>.
Example: As the <u>rain gently falls</u>,
        May my <u>heart soften</u>.
Example: As the <u>moon climbs in the sky</u>,
        May my <u>blessing expand</u>!
Example: As the <u>Bird sings</u>,
        May my <u>heart sing as well</u>.

Most people do not understand that there is a difference between imagination and imagery. Imagination by definition tells us something is not real. Therefore, to imagine something is to not create it. To imagine a world of peace will not create it. We must create the imagery of peace in our mind then embody it to create peace. It is similar to the concepts of faith and belief and how they differ. Faith is hoping for something that might be, trusting it will come about. Believing is accepting its reality, knowing it is real and going forward. Our reality or dream is created by our beliefs and the imagery we use to 'see' them. Remembering that imagery refers to not just visually seeing but to our feeling, hearing, smelling, tasting and memories.

One way to practice creating imagery is to begin by picking a topic: peace on earth, a more prosperous life, better relationships, or more fulfilling work for some examples. Pick one then take time to consider what you would like to be different. Then consider and focus on what you do want it to be like. Describe it to yourself. Speak about it using the Shamanic poetry techniques in the examples you have been given. At first it is a good idea to write it down, to refine the description. Later after you have had more practice you can just use your thoughts.

Ask yourself, "What does it (peace, prosperity, right relations) look like, feel like, sound like, smell like, or taste like? How would you feel if you were in peace, or prosperous, or in a right relationship? What are the others in this dream doing? How are you relating to others, and how are they relating to you?" Get as much detail as possible. Think of it as a movie and write the script, focusing on what you want, not what don't want. Use your feelings as well. When we create an image, we must see, hear and feel it. Use ALL your senses.

Continue to restate and reflect verbally this dream with the images of how it feels, sounds, and looks like. For example, after getting into a calm meditative state, think about a world at peace. "What does peace look like? What does peace smell like? What does it sound like? What does it feel like? What are others doing in a peaceful world? What are you doing in this peaceful world?"

After practicing this technique on various topics try another technique that is similar but more advanced. Begin by thinking of a situation in your life, positive or negative. First be grateful for it, 'see' it for what it is, then bless it and let it go. Then consider how this situation was constructed. Were you/are you the rescuer, victim, or perpetrator? Could you create a journey statement to shift your concept of the situation? Take time to reflect and observe it objectively. Now, considering whether you want to add to it or change it, go back and use the imagery technique to recreate or enhance it. As 'Children of the Sun', we are privileged to also enhance our good situation as well as change our disorganized ones.

After experiencing this method, move on to consider your life story. Write things down about it. What role are you playing? When do you take on that role and with whom? Can you find a recurring theme that might give you an idea of your wounds, like often being ignored, rejected, abandoned, negated, or imprisoned by religious belief? After time and reflection, while being the observer of this story, sit in meditation changing the past story into a journey statement. For example go from: I was abandoned by my father, to: I learned to be independent. From: I was raised in an oppressive church home, to: I learned to question what I was told. From: My parents expectations help me back, to: I embraced my personal power and found my own truth.

Now rewrite your life story, your future story, based on possibility. Consider all the possibilities you could have or create in this new life. Sit and do the imagery creating technique asking, "What does this new dream of all possibilities look like, feel like, sound like, smell like, taste like? How do others relate to you and each other in this new dream?" Consider only the possible future you would like to embrace, and contemplate that. It is a good idea with all these techniques to write them down for later reflection.

CHAPTER 11

The Vast Expansion
of Creation

O ur destiny is always available to us. As we recognize and embrace our timeless self, we will serve our entire species. As we heal, the world will heal, as we change, the world will change. From a healed state we are no longer guided by karma. It is then humanity will break free from what keeps us bound to strife and conflict. It is then as a collective we will evolve into Homo Luminous Beings. Our job is to heal ourselves and in doing so heal the world. To be like the Inka, Hopi, and Mayan elders who sat in meditation envisioning the world they want their grandchildren to inherit. A world in which the rivers and air are clean, there is food for all, and people live in peace with one another.

A Shaman is able to journey along a collective time line to find a more harmonious future, a possible future, no matter how improbable, where people live in harmony with nature, and peace with each other. The Sages of old call this 'dreaming the world into being'. This is the ultimate task of today's Shaman, to break free of the grip of fate, to no longer be the result of events that happened to us when we were children, in this life or our previous ones. When we track our destinies, we can choose who we're becoming, no longer trapped in who we've been. Our task today is not only to join the elders in meditation envisioning the possible future, but to clear the Hucha of the planet, and in doing so to serve the Mother. This is living the way of the Sage, and it is the way we become a Creator. It is the Sage that is able to create a dream of Beauty, to be in control of their personal dream. To become a Sage, we must perceive only beauty, remembering that everything experienced is a projection of the inner dream.

You are the Creator of each event and incident in your life. No one ever did or does anything to you without your consent. Remembering that, we begin to realize we do not need to fix anything in the outside world, only to transform ourselves on the inside. We do this by owning our projections, this changes them from within. Once we understand and accept that we can do this, we cease to be a helpless victim or an innocent bystander.

To interact with Creation, the domain of vibration and light, we practice conscious dreaming. The way to practice conscious dreaming is by allowing your mind to become silent, then entering the matrix of creation by journeying to the ninth chakra to become one with Spirit. Whatever we embody at this level prevails in our lives. Peace, serenity and abundance prevail in our lives when we embody them at this level of creation. In this Eagle level, we come to realize that nothing needs to be changed, that everything, in truth, is perfect in its own way. That is when we are free to change anything we wish, because we no longer have an investment in righting some wrong.

So often what we want to heal in our world is really what we are projecting onto it. If you are concerned about people in the world who are not free, consider first what within you is not free. When what is inside you is free, what is outside you can be liberated as well. This is the understanding that we are all one mind, and when we heal ourselves, we heal others.

Let us look at the mesa to understand the level of the Eagle, the level of creation. At the level of the Serpent, we try to change things by force. This is where most of society resides. At the level of the Jaguar, we try to change things through our will. This is the level most entrepreneurs and physicians work. At the level of the Hummingbird, we work to change things through visualization, words, prayers, and affirmations. This is where most healers and energy workers reside. But at the Eagle level we change things through dreaming by using imagery to program the mind in an altered or meditative state using feelings, sights, and sounds. Then holding in the mind that the image exists now, in the present, not in a future time we go to the ninth chakra and into the matrix of creation becoming one with the Creator. Connected to the source, in the matrix of creation, the dream that we have created with our mind then becomes reality. We change our vibration through imagery, see, feel, smell, and hear our desires as they would be in the present, then by being at the level of the Eagle, it is created.

When we step into this level, we must not attempt to define and control how what we want to create will manifest. When we attempt to define the details of manifestation, we change the vibration of what we want to create, to something that may appear in the future. By virtue of our attempt to organize the details, we are telling the Universe what we desire does not exist. It is no longer perceived in the present, but rather in the future. Instead, we must let the Universe take care of the details. We decide what we want, what it feels like, looks like, sounds like, and smells like, how we would relate to others, and how they would relate to us in this desired new dream. We make sure we are in a meditative state, that we have opened sacred space giving room for spiritual assistance, journey to the ninth chakra, then we let go. No concern about the how, when or where of the matter. We believe in that space that it is.

When we dream at this level of the Eagle we become one with Spirit, change our energetic vibration and attract that which vibrates in a similarly Divine manner.

It is difficult for us in the West to trust that we can achieve peace and happiness if we are not doing something active to bring it about. However, embodying peace and happiness does bring it about. Our egos do not want us to believe that we can have infinite power just by immersing ourselves in the wisdom of the Universe, but it is true. When we allow our ego to rule and insist that we must control the how of the events we end up in a constant struggle against the Universe. When you choose to simply be with the situation, whatever it is, not pushing it or willing or visualizing it, our very presence in non-resistance creates balance. As we become one with the situation and the energy, we are able to embody the new imagery we dreamed.

The energy of Divine Source resides in all things, including us. We can change whether it is raining or not when we understand that we are the rain because the same Divine Source resides in us both. We are connected with rain and can remember that at the level of Eagle. Change does not happen because you have forced it, commanded it, or visualized it, but because you become it. In sacred space, you remember yourself as rain and it appears in your reality or dream. You must be the rain, the peace, the prosperity you want to create in the world.

Yet, we must remember we cannot become the peace we wish to see until we own our projections. We must honestly see what we are putting out, the violence we project from within because of our own wounds, to truly change. We must remember what we create within, we create outward. We must clear our heart, clear our mind of the inner violence before we can become peace, prosperity, or rain within, and then create it without.

An important step to seeing our projections is to come to the realization that thoughts are different from ideas. Ideas occur to us. They come from a place of creation and power. Thought is the incessant brain chatter that is usually judgmental. Most thoughts are disguised memories of experiences that occurred in the early years of our lives, or former lifetimes. Every thought is a replay of a drama in which you were the victim, rescuer or perpetrator. Stop and identify them. Clear the thoughts by clearing the Hucha, or journey to find the source of the drama. Then by observing it, being with it, you can change it.

When you choose to simply be with the thoughts, whatever they are, your very presence in non-resistance creates balance. In this balance, healing or manifestation comes. Stop identifying with the thoughts. Instead ask yourself questions like, "Who is angry? Whose back is sore? Who is asking the question? Who is upset?" There you will find the Sage who will tell or show you the projection. You then come to realize that everything you believed to be real is a projection.

Also important to understand, so you can change your dream, is that real change comes by writing a new script, not editing the old one. We must stop editing our stories with the desire that 'if only it had been different' then trying to make it so. We cannot contemplate or wish or dream that a situation happened differently than it did. We must stop the denial, look at the story as it was or is, then turn it into a journey statement where we perceive what we gained rather than lost from the situation. Then we are free to rewrite our story as we choose from that point forward. Denial is such a difficult blockage. So often, we are able to see the dream or nightmare that others are trapped in much more easily than our own. Most of us can quickly perceive our friend is creating their own misery while still thinking our own grief is the result of some tragedy that befell us rather than our inability to stop trying to edit our scripts. Most of us are unable to do this because we are still unable to face our shadows. We have not learned that we can release it after we acknowledge it.

Our shadows are those parts of us that make us feel we are not good enough, not wanted, that we are a failure, or will never be happy. Projection is the mechanism through which we cast these undesirable qualities of our shadow onto others. We project every aspect of our shadow onto the world, be it positive or negative. In truth, everyone is a mirror for your own fearful projections. When we release our fear of the shadow allowing it to be what it is without judgment, we can let it go and move on to contemplate what we would like from life, dreaming it into reality.

Often, especially in psychology, people continue to feed their shadow with continual discussion or description, trapping them in the victim role. The more they own their shadow the bigger it gets. The constant reflecting, discussion, and questioning of their disempowering story keeps them trapped in the drama. They fall back into trying to rewrite the script instead of learning to create a new one. To dream a new reality for ourselves we must stop our constant reflecting, discussing, and questioning of our previous story plot. We must own and see the shadow, then using forgiveness let it go, change your story into a journey statement, use imagery to create a new dream, then journey to the ninth chakra to embody it.

Once you own your projections or shadow, if you are to dream the world differently, you must turn it into a story of power and grace. Write a new script called a journey statement, then stop remembering, or reflecting on the old script, or story. Let it go. Let it die.

For example if the old story says, "No one is ever happy, I can't be happy," the journey statement says, "As I make myself happy, everyone around me mirrors happiness back to me". Now you have asserted your power over your own happiness. If the old story is, "My children don't love me, or respect me," the journey statement says, "As I love and respect myself, I am able to love my children more fully, and they love and respect me in return." When the old thoughts, or shadow come up, you affirm the journey statement refusing to own the old script.

Because, if you know without a doubt that there is great poetry, grace and kindness within you the Universe will give you the opportunity to bring those attributes forth. If you know that you have the ability to allow others to be who they are, that you do not have to choose to be like them to allow them their own dream, you become free from them, from their emotional control.

Practice taking various disempowering stories and create journey statements. The disempowering story does not need to be yours, just practice dreaming and changing stories into journey statements.

A review: How do we create our dreams?

In summary, the way to prepare yourself to create your dream is to follow the way of the Sage. Perceive only beauty in everything, sit in meditation taking this beauty or desire to the ninth chakra level.

First we clear our hearts and minds to prepare. Start with deep breathing, clear your chakras and your Hucha, then get into a meditative state. Open sacred space, then personal sacred space. Use imagery to create a new script or dream, journey to the ninth chakra entering the Spirit or Creator level.

If you see other than beauty or feel stuck in your script, stop and use these steps. First, consider what the future is showing you or teaching you through your situation or current life dream. Then begin to discover and acknowledge the parts of this lesson, or situation you may have refused to look at. Own the projections. Ask yourself what you are placing on the situation that you don't like? Then free yourself from them with journey and observation. Practice 'no mind' or breaking free of your thoughts. Thoughts are usually negative dialogue that continues in our mind because we have not had closure with a past negative situation and they will continue through our mind until we acknowledge and release them. They can be understood as representing disguised past situations that need to be healed. Open yourself to ideas from the Universe. This is best done in meditation.

If your wounds or your current roles are still holding you in your old script, you can use the mesa's four-step process to help you transcend your roles and situations. Begin identifying, the quality of the Serpent asking, "What role do I play in this situation - victim, rescuer or perpetrator?" Next consider the quality of the Jaguar, and own the projection that is causing the story. Here we search for and acknowledge any fear associated with the denial of accepting our projections. Ask and find why we cling to the idea that we are not responsible for our situations, that we are not the ones that need to change. Then use integration, the quality of the Hummingbird and turn 'the story' into a journey statement to learn from it so you can move on. Remember, a journey statement is where you find a way to comment or accept a situation in a way that reflects on what positive attribute you have gained. Transcendence, or the quality of the Eagle, is last. It is where you contemplate or see opportunity or possibility where you once only saw probability. You ask what the possibilities are, then use imagery to experience various possibilities. See them as they exist in the now. You can write, speak, draw, sing, or dance the images if that helps you. If you are still unsure about dreaming or how to own the ability, journey and ask to be shown by your Power Animals or guides.

Now with a cleared heart and mind go back into meditation, consciously dreaming by imaging what you want your dream, your world, or situation to be like. Feel it, see it, hear it, smell it, taste it. Create the imagery. Be the rain! Image what the best possibility could be and feel it, be there. Then let it go. Do not dwell on it. Honor your work, and embrace the new reality. Spend time being grateful for the change because gratitude manifests new desires. Occasionally throughout the day, if the old thought comes to you, embody that new dream, be peace, or abundance, or happiness. When you get a snag, question the Sage within, "Who is mad? Who is unhappy? Who will not be grateful?"

Changing the dream is easiest when we master our concept of time, a function of the frontal lobes or God brain. Let go of the idea that effect follows cause. This is the way to step into the stream of timelessness, to step out of linear time and into sacred time. Contemplate circular time remembering that the main operating principle in sacred time is synchronicity or the serendipitous occurrence of events. Synchronicity allows for future causation. It is more interested in the purpose and meaning of an event than in its present or past cause. "What is the meaning and purpose of the event?" is asked considering the synchronicity of the event. For example, looking at a situation where a frail, fearful child terrified of bulls grows up to become a bullfighter, using the cause and effect concept, a psychologist might explain the reason for his vocational choice was to prove he was a brave man. Looking at his life moving through linear time it was said he grew up to compensate. But looking at his life through the concept of Shamanic circular time, it could be argued that the boy had a knowing he would be facing huge bulls in a ring one day which gave him reason to be frightened as a child.

When open to the concept of circular time, we can reflect that it is possible that things we felt had 'blocked' us or 'stopped' us were really a knowing from our future. Maybe the stop lights happen not to upset you or to cause you to be late, but because you were avoiding a possible future accident. We can then contemplate the possibility that the future, not our past is creating our present. We are what we are, because of what we are becoming, not because of what we have been or were in the past. When we trust that the unscheduled events of our lives are a form of Spiritual direction, we open our mind to mastering the concept of time allowing us to easily manifest the dream of our choice. If you are still unsure about dreaming, or how to own the ability, journey and ask to be shown by your Power Animals or guides.

CHAPTER 12

The Despacho, Ceremony of Ayni or Reciprocity

Remember, also, that this path is about respect.
– Fredy "Puma" Quispe Singona

Shaman of all cultures use ceremony to connect with Divine Source. The Despacho Ceremony is the main ceremony performed by the Peruvian Shaman for the health and well-being of the people. It is an ancient, beautiful ceremony still practiced in Peru. It is done to express gratitude and to manifest what we would like to attract into our lives or into the lives of our family or community members. It gives the Shaman a symbolic way to show gratitude, love and respect for Mother Earth as well as the great Nature Spirits of the mountains, lakes and rivers. When we express love and gratitude, we attract more of what it is we are grateful for, we manifest our intentions. The Despacho is also used to celebrate weddings, birth, or healing.

The participants, in a more western style ceremony, or the Shaman in a more traditional style ceremony create an art piece similar to a mandala as an act of love and gratitude, as a symbol of Ayni. This art piece is made of natural and man-made products that symbolize the requests of the participants to the realm of spiritual power. This piece of art serves as an offering of gratitude to the Pachamana (Mother Earth), and to the Apus (Mountain Spirits). After the art is created, the Shaman burns or buries the bundle releasing the prayers and requests, dispatching them to the Spirits. Despacho ceremonial bundles are typically addressed to the larger forces of nature: Pachamama (Mother Earth), Apukuna (Mountain Spirits), Chaskakuna (the Stars), or Inti (the Sun).

Despacho Ceremonies are performed as a form of Ayni or reciprocity with the Universe. The concept of Ayni is central to Andean Shamanism and is based on a mutual dependency between humans, nature, and spiritual forces. Ayni brings balance into our lives creating right relationship between the secular and sacred worlds. Andean metaphysics teaches that human health and well-being depend on balanced reciprocity between all elements of life. Therefore, when soliciting an outcome from the Spirits, our exchange is done using our energy to create beauty in an art piece that we infused with prayers and appreciation then give to the Spirits in gratitude.

Despachos can be performed in and for groups, cities and countries, or for individuals. The intention behind a Despacho Ceremony can range from something as noble as world peace, to something as down to earth as offering thanks for a bountiful harvest, or for something as personal as relief from joint pain. You could even include prayers for all three in one Despacho Ceremony! A personal Despacho Ceremony can focus on any areas of your life where you feel you need support or would like to ask for blessings. It is a powerful way to set your intentions, then letting them go out into the Universe to be manifested. You may be surprised to recognize in the weeks and months following a Despacho Ceremony that you are indeed receiving the things you asked for, though perhaps in an unexpected way or unusual form. The Universe often gives to us in a way more appropriate or powerful than you could have dreamed of on your own.

To create a Despacho, begin by clearing the participants and the space where you will create your Despacho with sacred sage smudge. Open with prayer, then call in the directions creating a Sacred Space.

Next open your personal sacred space over the area where you plan to create your Despacho and over the prepared items you plan to use. On a large piece of white paper you will create your Despacho with various items which will represent your desires, and requests. Also included in your art piece are your prayers and offerings.

Prayers and requests are then blown into 'kintus', a set of three leaves which represent the three worlds and placed in the art piece. The offerings to the Spirits are presented in the form of food or decorations you place on the Mandala. They represent what you may be requesting or giving thanks for.

When you have finished your Despacho take time to admire it, and feel a sense of completion. Then folding it, close it into a package tying it up with a string. If you have a mesa, set the Despacho package on it and breathe a final blessing into the package as you hold it up to the sky, and down to the earth. Next, take the Despacho package off your Mesa and brush the body of the participants and yourself with it. This will release Hucha from the participants into the bundle which is also an offering or a gift for the Mother Earth. The package is then taken and either burned for quick results or buried for a slower easier shift. If you burn the Despacho package, do not look at it while it is burning but allow the Spirits to do their work in private. If you bury it, leave it and do not return. Usually more prayers, drumming and celebration follow to end the Ceremony. Remember to close your personal space and the sacred space when you are finished with your ceremony. Usually there is a small celebration after.

Creating a Despacho bundle

Main items to gather prior to creation of a Despacho:

1. Large white paper approximately 16 by 20 inches folded into thirds both ways to make nine squares when reopened.
2. Sugar, both in the form of candy and white granulated sugar.
3. A clam shell to represent the Great Mother.

4. Enough local leaves to make eight or more kintu sets (a set is three leaves). Kintus are usually made of coca leaves but in Northern America it is acceptable to substitute oak leaves, bay leaves, or other leaves native to the area.

5. Plants, food, minerals, animal products or man–made symbols; items that represent your requests or intentions.

6. A small wooden cross to represent the male energy.

7. Flowers, red for the Mother Earth and white for the mountain or Apu Spirits.

8. Small bowl of red wine, and small bowl of chicha (corn beer) or vodka.

9. String to tie the bundle. I like to use multicolored yarn.

Building a Despacho:

1. Begin by smudging yourself and the participants, then pray, and open sacred space. If you have a mesa you could open it to connect to your personal power before you begin to create the Despacho.

2. Next, open and lay out the folded white paper. Put small amounts of sugar in the four corners, then make a large X from corner to corner through the center of your middle square of the paper with sugar.

3. Lay the clam shell in the middle or center of the paper then place the cross in the shell. This is to represent a balance of the male and female energy.

4. Offer kintus, a set of three leaves to each participant. Then lead the participants in blowing their prayers and intentions into them as they move to face each direction, including the earth and the heavens. Ask for the assistance of the four directions during this time, as well. When finished with the prayers, the kintus are returned to the leader (Shaman) of the ceremony who places them in a circle around the shell. They may be placed on the Despacho by the participants

themselves, but this is usually only done with participants that have an understanding of what they are doing. Traditionally eight kintu sets are used for a Despacho when it is dedicated to the Pachamama, feminine energy or the Earth. A circle of twelve kintu sets are used on the Despacho when it is dedicated to the male aspect of the Divine, the Apu Spirits. More sets of kintus may be used if you feel led to do that. Even a small circle of kintu sets, a large circle, or two circles of kintu sets may be placed on the paper. Use your discretion and what feels right to you. It often depends on how many participants are present for the ceremony.

5. After the Kintu sets are placed, further items that represent the intentions, or requests are added to the Mandala. These requests may be voiced or requested in silence. Voicing the intentions give more power. Some examples of items of intent are: candies or cookies, sweet things, to show love and respect to the Great Mother; rice or grain for continued nourishment, cotton balls or marshmallows to represent the clouds and to connect to the world of Spirit; gold foil to represent the masculine energy of the Sun, or silver foil to represent the feminine energy of the Moon; multicolored confetti or paper streamers to represent joy; gold fish crackers to represent abundance and prosperity; spices for the fullness and beauty of life; animal cracker cookies to honor the animal kingdom and our Power Animals; flowers for the Beauty Way, and to honor the Earth and the Sun!

6. The "ingredients" or items of intention vary according to the purpose of the Despacho. They are chosen to represent what the participants want to manifest or communicate to the Divine. A drawing of a desire, like a new home, photos of happy couples for good relationships, a toy bride and groom for a successful marriage, or monopoly money for a larger income can also be placed in the art piece. Feel free to use your creative energy, remembering to mentally or verbally state your intention when placing them in the Despacho.

7. Flowers may then be placed on the Despacho adding to the art work. Then a circle made with string is used to circle around the edge of the art piece to enclose the energy. I use colored yarn to represent the rainbow and the Beauty Way.

8. The leader then dips a flower head into wine and shakes the liquid on to the Despacho to represent the blood of the mother. This is done again in vodka or chica beer to represent the strength of the father.

9. More prayers, admiration of the art piece, and discussion or comments on the desires or new dream can be shared in the group at this time. Often, a journey or time for contemplation is appropriate here as well. When it feels complete and right, the Despacho is closed. The Shaman folds the paper into a 'package' which holds the offerings inside like a wrapped gift and ties it with string. If you have opened your mesa, you may close it at this time and lay the package on top of the mesa, but this is optional.

10. The Shaman or leader then takes the bundle and breathes the intention into it, a blessing for a wedding, a request for health, prosperity, closure for a divorce, the sale of your home, whatever the Despacho was created for is breathed into the package. The leader or Shaman then takes the Despacho package and 'sweeps' the body of the participants with it. Brushing down the legs, arms, back, and across the shoulders of each participant. Do this on both the front and back of the body, then tap the third eye, heart chakra, and the second chakra or navel area. This 'sweeping' clears the Hucha from the participant's body, putting it into the Despacho package as part of the gift for the Spirits.

11. Remember to close your personal sacred space, then the larger sacred space when you finish your ceremony, ending with a prayer.

12. At this time, celebrating with drumming, songs, or feasting is appropriate. While the participants are celebrating, to finish the ceremony the Shaman or leader takes the package and

burns it for quick results or will bury it for a slower change. Sometimes this is done while the participants are left to the feast, but if it is just the Shaman and one or two participants they may go with the Shaman for the burning. Take the extra wine and vodka and pour it on the package before burning it, or pour it on top of where you bury the package as a gift to the Earth.

13. Tell the participants or clients not to look at the burning package if they are near the burn site. The Spirits eat the Hucha in the package and do not want to be watched. Let your desires go. The Spirits will handle your requests in their own way.

14. If the Shaman is not able to bury or burn the bundle at this time, the package may be placed and left on the Shamans mesa until able to do so.

Despacho Offering Suggestions

A short list of the possible meanings of items
to be used as Despacho offerings.
Add to or substitute other items that could
also have a similar interpretation.

COPAL: Offering to the Lower World, the Shadow
FRANKINCENSE: Offering to the Upper World, the Light
PALO SANTO: Holds Space for our Prayers
COCA: Sacred Wisdom of the Mother
TOBACCO: Offering to the Sky Father
SAGE: Purification, Banishment of the Negative

PLANTS AND FOODS
ANISE: Celebration & the Senses
BERRIES: Rewards, Fruits of Labor
CEDAR: Wisdom of the Forest
CORN: A Gift of the Earth, Our Daily Sustenance
CORNMEAL: Offering to the Earth Mother
COTTON: Dreams, Clouds, Mountain Snows
FIGS: Ancient Mountain Spirits
FLOWERS: The Beauty of Nature & The Power of Light
GARLIC: Absorption of the Negative, Banishment
GRAINS: Sustenance, Abundance
LAVENDER: Purity, Purification
LAUREL: Sacredness, Victory over Adversity
LEAVES: Honoring Nature Spirits
LIMA BEANS: Sacred Places and Power Spots
LIQUOR: High Energy, Honoring the Spirit World, Our Ancestors
PEANUTS: Caves, Places for Elemental Spirits
POLLEN: Offering to all Living Creatures
RAISINS: Offering to the Dead
RICE: Nourishment, Offerings to the Spirit World

SWEETS: Fertility, Beginnings, Potential
SUGAR: Sweetness, Feeding the Spirits
VEGETABLE OIL: The Nourishing Power of Nature
WINE, RED: Honoring the Mother, Menstrual Blood
WINE, WHITE: Honoring the Moon, Fluids of Purification

MAN-MADE SYMBOLS & SYMBOLS
ALPHABET NOODLES: Language of the Soul, The Unwritten
ASHES: Offering to Our Personal Ancestors
BEARS: Personal Power
BUTTERFLIES: Happiness, Spontaneity
CANDLES: Celebrations & Rejoicing
CANDY: Compassion & Love
CIRCLES: Completion, Good Luck
CONFETTI: Happiness, Celebrations
COINS: Good Fortune, Wealth
IMAGES OF COUPLES: Marriage, Love, Reproduction
CROSSES: Decisions, Coming Together
DICE: Good Luck
FISH: Abundance, Prosperity
FLUTES: Voices of the Ancestors
FROGS: Keepers & Guardians of the Waters
GOLD LEAF: Wisdom, Direct Knowledge from Nature
SILVER LEAF: Intuition, Clairvoyance, Message from the Moon
GOLD THREAD: Connection to the Earth Mother
HANDS: Sensitivity, Mastery
HEARTS: Working from Love, From the Center

ANIMAL PRODUCTS
ANIMAL SHAPES: Honoring Animal Kingdom, Power Animals
FAT: Purest form of energy
BONE: Inner Core, Structure, Connection to Animal Relatives
CORAL: Diplomacy, Quiets the Emotions, Intuition
EGGS: The Unborn, Purity, Healing
FEATHERS: Connection to Birds & Native American Wisdom

133

FUR: Boundaries, Our Relations in Nature
HUMAN HAIR: Honoring our Connection to the Animal World
MILK: Connection to the Mother, Honoring Trees
PEARLS: Infinite Wisdom & Purity
STARFISH: Foundations, Successful New Beginnings
SEAHORSE: Delicacy & Balance
SHELLS: Power of the Waters: Depth, Faith, Flexibility

MINERALS – SOME OF THESE WORK BEST WHEN BURYING THE DESPACHO

GOLD: Masculine, The Sun, Insight
SILVER: Feminine, The Moon, Intuition
AGATE: Acceptance, Balance, Raises Consciousness
AMBER: Protection, Memory, Calming
AMETHYST: Higher Knowledge, Insight, Protection
AVENTURINE: Joy, Mental Clarity, Positive Attitudes
BLOODSTONE: Blood & Heart Healing, Vitality, Courage
CALCITE: Astral Projection, Balances Yin/Yang qualities
CARNELIAN: Protection against Envy, Banishes Sorrow
CITRINE: Relationships, Confidence, Protection, Wealth
COPPER: The Earth's Gift, Conductivity
DIAMOND: Removes Blockages, Balances the Mind, Power
FLUORITE: Ability to Perceive Higher Levels of Reality
GARNET: Circulation, Stimulates Imagination, Willpower,
HEMATITE: Protection, Aids Astral Projection, Self-Esteem
HERKIMER: Cleanses Subtle Bodies, Past-life Memory
IRON: Strength, Persistence, Endurance, Direction
JADE: Good Luck & Prosperity, Divine Love, Protection
LODESTONE: The Power to Attract & Bind Together
MOONSTONE: Open to Feminine Qualities, Clairvoyance
OBSIDIAN: Removes Obstacles & Negativity, Prophetic Vision
OPAL: Protection, Cosmic Consciousness & Intuition
PERIDOT: Clarity, Patience, Clairvoyance, Wealth
PYRITE: Material Realization, Good Fortune, Eases Anxiety
CLEAR QUARTZ: Purity of Perception, Intention, Amplification

ROSE QUARTZ: Love & Romance, Opens Heart, Forgiveness
SMOKEY QUARTZ: Purification, Eliminates Shadow, Grounding
RUTILATE QUARTZ: Breaks Old Patterns, Childhood Blockages
RHODOCHROSITE: Cleanses Subconscious, Self-Identity
RUBY: Spiritual Balance, Heart Healing, Confidence, Leadership
SALT: Protection, Boundaries
SAPPHIRE: Communication with Spirit Guides, Telepathy
TIGER EYE: Separates Desire from Need, Right Action
TOURMALINE: Protection, Dispels Negativity, Fear & Grief
TURQUOISE: Healing, Protection, Strength

CHAPTER 13

Andean Metaphysical Cosmology

A Shaman is different from a priest, sorcerer or witch-doctor. A Shaman is an individual who has had a mystical experience that brings them to a higher perceptual state where they can perceive the totality and cycles of life. They can modify their state of consciousness and journey at will to the lower worlds to learn the causes of people's illnesses or misfortunes, or to the upper worlds to affect the future. Such trances can be induced by the ingestion of hallucinogenic substances, like Ayahuasca or chewing the leaves of the sacred Coca plant, both used widely by the Indian Shaman of Peru. However, in today's world with education and through the Rites, it is no longer necessary to use mind altering substances to successfully learn to journey. In today's world our energy is lighter and we have more knowledge and information of the esoteric. Drumming or rattling usually alters the mind enough to allow today's Shaman to successfully journey for Divine revelation without using hallucinogenic drugs. I base that knowing on my own personal experience, and that of other Shamanic practitioners that have no need for substances to do their healing work.

In the western world we base our perceptions around laws and rules. The Andean thought is one of concepts, where a Shaman works to change the world by changing their idea or concepts of it, not find or shift the rules that are believed to govern it. The Earth based philosophy of the Andean is one of inclusion. They do not have the belief that they were banished from the Garden by the Divine Source. They still live in the Garden and that is why they have no trouble talking to the Divine in nature. The Andean Shaman also uses the Inca medicine wheel or mesa as the four steps to healing.

The Peruvian Q'ero metaphysical cosmology, and the larger Andean sacred tradition, is both mystical and Shamanic. Shaman enter an altered state of consciousness at will to travel through a multi-dimensional Universe and retrieve information for predictions, healing, and insight. They journey for information, using drumming, or other techniques to induce the altered state. Usually they undertake the Spirit journey as a specific ritual for a well-defined purpose and a particular outcome.

Mystics' spiritual pursuits are solitary. Their goal is to experience a profoundly personal transcendental integration with the natural world, the larger ground of being. The ego is overcome, the boundary between self and other dissolves, and one experiences Unity consciousness. Mystics are usually not associated with rituals or seeking an outcome.

The Andean Shaman is both mystic and Shamanic. They undergo formal initiation into their metaphysical work. They perform ritual for an intended purpose and commune with nature spirits with the intent of receiving guidance from them. However, the Q'ero Andean practice is fundamentally much more mystical than Shamanistic. They do not usually employ drumming or ecstatic dancing or use psychotropic drugs to induce altered states. Instead they develop their energy body. They learn to interchange energy with the Kawsay Pacha, the cosmos of living energy. Their goal is to always be in Ayni, or reciprocity, with all the other energies of the Kawsay Pacha. Therefore, they seek mystical union more than Shamanic control of the multidimensional world of energy. These metaphysicians blend mystical practices with Shamanic worldviews which are expressed in their concept of harmonizing the left and right sides of the mesa.

The three worlds of the Inkan Cosmos are called: Ukhupacha, the Lower World, the place of the subconscious or unconscious, of dreams and intuition, ruled by Huascar, and symbolized by the Serpent. Kaypacha, the Middle World, the physical Earth, the mundane, everyday world and awareness, ruled by Quetzalcoatl, symbolized by the Jaguar. Hanaqpacha, the Upper World, the place of the most refined energies, the world of spiritual being and the super conscious, ruled by Pachakuti, symbolized by the Condor. Interestingly, these three worlds seem to correspond with the Holy Trinity; the Father, Son and Holy Spirit seen in Christianity, as well as the Body/Mind/Spirit idea seen in Eastern Religions.

A Chakana is a three stepped symmetric cross with a hole in the center of it. It represents the Southern Cross constellation believed by the ancient Andeans to be the center of the Universe. The Southern Cross (Crux) is comprised of four main stars, each corresponding to the cardinal points of the compass. It is one of the most distinct constellations viewed from the Southern Hemisphere. This Chakana or Inka cross symbolizes what is known in other mythologies as the World Tree, or the Tree of Life. The word is derived from the Quechua traditional language of the Inka from the word 'Chakay' which means to bridge or to cross. This stepped cross is made up of an equal-armed cross indicating the cardinal directions superimposed on a square that represents two other levels of existence. It is a symbol of the three worlds: Hanaqpacha, the upper world inhabited by the superior gods; Kaypacha, the world of our everyday existence; and the Ukupacha, the underworld.

The Chakana also represents the Shaman's ability to travel to these three various levels of existence. The hole through the centre of the cross is the axis, the pathway the Shaman uses to travel to the other levels of existence. It also represents Cuzco, the center of the Inka Empire.

The Inka had a calendar that was composed of twelve months, each with thirty days. Each month had its own festival. Some speculate that the twelve corners of the Chakana cross represented this twelve month cycle, with the four major arms of the cross representing the points of a compass. The Chakana not only represents within its design the four directions: North, South, East and West, but also the four elements of Earth, Air, Water, and Fire. The top of the cross is said to represent God, or Wiracocha, the highest level of consciousness expressed as the Great Spiritual Central Sun. Mother Earth or Pachamama anchors the bottom of the cross bringing alignment to the equal armed cross.

This Chakana symbol is found throughout the Andes and can be seen in the architectural designs on many buildings, temples and ancient monuments, such as at the Temple of the Condor in Machu Picchu. It is also used as a talisman, a symbol that protects the wearer from harm and brings good luck.

Even today, the people of Peru and Bolivia honor the Southern Cross or Chakana each year on the third of May. May is the month of harvest and during this celebration people give thanks to the cross, the constellation for the protection of their crops. The Chakana, when used in meditation or in teaching, is said to bring spiritual balance and deeper insight into the many levels of consciousness.

CHAPTER 14

Journey - A Shaman's Greatest Tool!

"The journey is about you right now, not about anybody else asking
for your help. The most important tool to use is the new found ability
to say yes to your calling and no to the things that will distract you."
- Alberto Villoldo

Shaman is often described as someone who travels to the
Spirit world or alternate realities to retrieve power, energy
and wisdom that can be used for the betterment of the self
or the world. They call upon the essential forces of nature such as:
the winds, sacred plants, smoke, rocks, animals, fire, rivers, and the
breath for healing. They call in helping Spirits, exorcise harmful
intrusions and balance energies through the vibration of drums, bells,
rattles, movement, chanting and other methods. They are connected
to something greater than themselves, something that flows through
them and all things. Not that everyone is not connected to this same
force, but the Shaman is aware of this connection. The main way
they access the Spirit world is through journey.

Anthropologists found that Shaman in cultures separated by
thousands of miles and without knowledge of each other developed
healing and ceremonial approaches that were almost identical. This

can only be explained by the journey. All Shaman journey to the same source or Universal field for information so it is logical they would often be given the same information since it is from the same Source.

A journey is similar to a guided meditation, but connects you to the essential force, assisting you in accessing Divine revelation. It is usually done using a drum or a rattle for easier access to an altered state. The Shaman is usually assisted by a Power Animal or guide when they journey and there are many stylistic ways to do journey that are effective. Most Shaman or healers have their own unique ways although they are usually similar. There is no real right or wrong way, and after you have been doing journey for a while it will shift to suit the need. What is important is effectiveness. If it is effective, then it is right.

Below is how I guide or lead people through journeys when teaching them how to journey, or when working with them to heal themselves. Following this order seems to help people not only heal, but learn in a most effective way. You can follow this same pattern for yourself in your personal journey as well.

Basic Outline for all Journeys

To Journey: First set your intention, on what you or your client wants from this journey: to find a Power Animal, to meet the elements or archetypes, to realize or see your wounds, to get an answer to a question, to see a past life, to find closure, to find a missing soul part, to be open to a message relevant to your situation, to find your soul contracts and renegotiate them...you get the point.

Begin by opening a sacred space calling in the directions, then open your personal sacred space. Using a drum, a CD of drum music, a friend that can drum for you, or shaking a rattle, get comfortable and listen to the drum or rattle while breathing in a way that will take you into a meditative or relaxed state.

Continuing to listen to the drum, begin to see or imagine walking on a dirt road, coming to a forest, go into the forest, then getting deeper into the forest. Make sure you engage your senses feeling, seeing and hearing the landscape. When you are ready, break out of the forest into a field, find a large tree in the middle of the field and sit by it. From here the journey is different depending on the need. If you or the client needs to contact a lost relative for closure, to connect with an element, an archetype or a Power Animal, call to them, and observe them come from over a hill to the left of the tree. Make sure you or your client is grounded, and sees themselves in a bubble of protective light before calling to the aspect you want to connect with. Usually Divine Source will guide you from there, be open to guidance.

To find past lives, wounds, get major revelation, or renegotiate your contracts takes a little more. You must go into the lower world. To do this, when sitting or standing by the tree, notice a small animal hole at the base of the tree. Then jump into the hole with abandonment, free falling down, tumbling and rolling safely, then landing at the bottom, tumbling out onto the ground. Then rise and find a bench to sit on. From here the journey can vary depending on the need, or how you are moved when guiding someone. You can have them (or you) ask, questions, or call a Power Animal to take them (or you) on a journey. Or you may walk to a large stone by a stream to look into a pool to see your past lives. If you are journeying on your own, Divine Source will take over and guide you, you will not have to control the journey, but rather just be open to the experience. The guided portion is usually just for training, or to assist someone who is new to journey.

When you are ready to return, or for them to return from the journey, go back to the bench, then back to the hole you/they tumbled out of, thank any Power Animals or elements that assisted you then jump up back through the hole, feeling yourself flying upward, then tumbling out from the animal hole and back to the base of the tree in the middle world. Take a moment to ground and clear the energy. This is easily done by resting against, or placing a hand on the tree and feeling its life force energy flow through you or the client. Rise and walk back through the field to the forest, through the forest then exit to the road. Continue to walk down the dirt road, coming back to the place your physical body is resting. Reenter the body. Let the drum do five strong beats at least three times to make sure all energy has returned to the body, and to signal the end of the journey. Close your personal space, close the sacred space.

Do not be concerned if things happened differently for you than what is laid out in the journey example. Just go with what is given. This is just a formula, or a skeleton to follow. Be open to however your journey unfolds and to what you were given during it. When journeying on your own, the formula will help you to get started, but usually the journey will be very unique. As long as you open sacred space, ask for assistance, then thank the Universe when you are finished closing sacred space, it is all good. All journey work can be adapted to get answers to questions, meet the archetypes, your personal Power Animal or your personal guide, even to go with your Power Animal on a special journey. It can be used as a template for many uses. Be open to how it unfolds as often the psyche or your higher self may have plans of its own, always for our highest good. Do take time to write the journey down after the experience. Sometimes it takes a while for us to understand the message we received and we may forget what we saw, so write it down.

No matter what style of energy work, Shamanism or even magical practice you do, to be effective, you must develop a relationship with the subconscious mind and the other worlds. It is the journey that formally connects you to the elements, archetypes, Power Animals, and guides. It starts your relationship with them so you will be able to call on their assistance when you need them. All elements, archetypes, Power animals, and guides are but representative of the One Great Power. When you are communicating and thanking them you are speaking directly to Source. It is through humility we grow more powerful. It is by showing respect and communicating you will be able to harness allies in a cooperative relationship. For the most productive results let go of resistance and merge with them. They can teach us to be more fully integrated with the powers that surround us, if we ask. They give us direct knowledge as we learn to work with them.

Chapter 15

Appendix – Important Extras

Short Explanation of the Munay-Ki Rites.

We call the first ceremonial energetic connection the Healer Rite because it connects the receiver to a lineage of Earthkeepers or healers. These Earthkeepers assist the receiver in personal healing and transformation by awakening the receiver's ability to heal themselves and others in a gentle energetic way. They work to heal the wounds of the past as well as those inherited from the receiver's ancestors.

We call the second ceremonial energetic connection the Bands of Power. These bands are protections installed in your Luminous Energy Field or aura that represent the elements: Earth, Water, Fire, Air and Spirit. They act as filters or deflectors breaking down misaligned energies that daily come our way, allowing us to dismantle unhealthy emotional and psychological protections we created in our past.

We call the third ceremonial energetic connection the Harmony Rite. In this initiation, the energy of seven archetypal energies arc placed in your chakras as seeds balancing your energy body and chakra system. The seeds help to clear the psychic sludge that has built up in the chakras over time, including past lives. The seven archetypes are: the four organizing principles of the universe: Serpent, Jaguar,

Hummingbird, Condor or Eagle, and the three luminous beings or archangels: Huascar, Quetzalcoatl, and Pachakuti.

We call the fourth ceremonial energetic connection the Seer Rite because this ceremony gives the receiver the ability to see their own projections. This initiation connects the visual cortex, at the back of your head, to the third eye and heart chakra allowing the receiver to see from their heart. I personally believe this is the most powerful energetic ceremony. When we begin to 'see' our projections, those parts of yourself and others you have not previously seen, then healing on a deep level begins. It is after this ceremony that we begin to become aware of our original wound, and are able to clear it with the awareness of it. This is the key to our personal healing.

We call the fifth ceremonial energetic connection the Daykeeper Rite. It is the first lineage ceremony and connects you to Masters from the past that tended ancient altars. It gives the ability to call upon the power of these ancient altars to heal and bring balance to any situation. Places where ceremony for healing and power are used accumulate positive energy. To be able to access these altars, or healing places through ceremony and journey, gives us more power and positive energy to accomplish our intentions. The power of this initiation, in my mind, is that it begins the process of healing the inner feminine giving us the ability to access the power of the Divine Feminine.

We call the sixth ceremonial lineage energetic connection the Wisdomkeeper Rite. A Wisdomkeeper protects the ancient medicine teachings and shares them with others only when appropriate. This ceremony begins the process of healing the inner masculine. It is the purpose of the Divine Masculine energy to protect life, the ultimate purpose of all males. Sadly, in the current world of humanity, male energy has confused that call to protect and care with the need to use violence to rescue or accomplish goals. What I have observed also, is if male energy is not able to battle or use violence for what it believes is right and just, it often turns that violence upon its self or loved ones. I believe this confusion comes from the wounds the male energy carries. After this important ceremony, we are able to begin to step outside of time and heal the wounds from all of our former lifetimes, and step out of the triangle of disempowerment healing our personal inner masculine's wounds.

The Mountains have always been regarded as places of power and wisdom, where mankind meets the Divine. This lineage also has a close connection to the Apus or Mountain Spirits and after being connected to this ancient lineage of Wisdomkeepers we are able to call upon these mountains, these high places for help and assistance.

We call the seventh ceremonial energetic connection the Earthkeepers Rite. It connects the receiver to the guardians of our galaxy who understand that every action and every thought that each person on the planet has effects humanity. They are stewards of all life on the Earth and the receiver comes under the protection of these Luminous Beings after this initiation. Being connected to them gives us the ability to call on their power when we need it. After this ceremony, the receiver will begin to develop a body that heals, ages and dies differently. They learn more about the way of being a seer and begin to be able to help others dream their world into being.

We call the eighth ceremonial energetic connection the Starkeeper Rite. It anchors the receiver safely to all life, the future as well as the present. The power in this transmission is that it connects us to the Star Beings, to our original ancestors. The Andean Inka culture live very close to the stars on the mountain tops and they believe humans came from the stars. This ceremony is said to slow down the aging process and make us more resistant to disease.

We call the ninth ceremonial energetic connection the Creator Rite because receiving this transmission further awakens the ability to dream all of Creation into being. After this ceremony the receiver becomes a conduit between the manifest and un-manifest worlds. Until the Inka Elders first gifted this Rite to outsiders, few people were able to attain this level of initiation, the ability to travel to the field of all possibility. Now with this ceremony many are able to awaken their Consciousness fully.

It is my belief that all these ceremonial energetic connections correlate with the chakras, and the seven initiations of the spiritual path that all humans make. Everyone is on a spiritual journey whether they acknowledge it or not. Some people are doing it the hard way, and some are taking an easier path, both are a matter of choice and free will. These ceremonies are a fast track through the initiations because we have the assistance of the Masters they connect us to. The eighth and ninth ceremony are especially powerful and special because they connect us to the place of our origin, the stars, and allow us to travel to the great field of all possibility.

CREATING SACRED SPACE FOR CEREMONY OR HEALINGS

Smudging

It is important to smudge the area and the participants before any ceremony or healing. This will clear the area and the participants of Hucha and set them in a sacred mental space. If you know some of your participants are sensitive to smoke, or the facility you are holding your ceremony in may be concerned about you smudging, you can buy a liquid sage spray to use.

Opening Prayer

Great Spirit whose voice we hear in the wind, hear our prayer. We come before you today for ceremony, asking that all things unfold according to your will.

Invoking each direction

Face each direction, one at a time, rattling or holding up your hand, call out loud with authority to each direction. Examples of what to say to each direction are below. Eventually you will speak from your heart. Just remember what each direction represents and what they can do for you when you call to them, this will help you speak from your heart.

South

To the Winds of the South, Great Serpent, wrap your coils of light around us. Teach us to shed the past the way you shed your skin, to walk softly on the Earth. Teach us the Beauty Way.

West

To the Winds of the West, Mother Jaguar, Protect our medicine space. Teach us the way of peace, to live impeccably, show us the way beyond death, to step beyond fear and violence, to become warriors without enemies.

North

To the Winds of the North, Hummingbird, grandmother and grandfathers, Ancient Ones, help us to make our spiritual journey to wholeness. Connect us to the wisdom of the ancestors. We honor you who have come before us, and you who will come after us, our children's children.

East

To the Winds of the East, Great Eagle, Condor, come to us from the place of the rising Sun. Show us the mountains we only dare to dream of, let us fly wing to wing with the Great Spirit, so we may see from a higher perspective. Thank you for teaching us to create a new dream for ourselves.

Below

Mother Earth, we've gathered for the healing of all of your children – the Stone people, the Plant people, the four-legged, the two-legged, the creepy crawlers, the finned, the furred and the winged ones, all our relations. Thank you for supporting us, and giving us life. We give you all our misaligned energy so that you in reciprocity will give us abundance, healing and balance. Help us to continue to walk in Beauty.

Above

Father Sun, Grandmother Moon and the Star Nations above – Great Spirit, you who are known by a thousand names, and you who are the unnamable one, we call to you. Thank you for bringing us together and allowing us to sing the song of life. Bring us your light and energy so we may continue on the path of the Beauty Way that we may return to balance, health and wholeness.

Ending

After the ceremony or healing, remember to close sacred space by thanking each direction. Holding up your hand toward one at a time, thank them for their presence and assistance.

OPENING THE WIRACOCHA

Wiracocha is the name of the Peruvian God of Creation and was chosen by Alberto Gonzales and his mentor Don Antonio Morales as the Munay-Ki term for the eighth or Soul Star Chakra that rests above your head.

The name Wiracocha mean 'source of the sacred' or 'foam on the ocean'. When this eighth chakra is fully awakened it is said to shine like a radiant sun inside the Luminous Energy Field. The Wiracocha can be opened enveloping you to create a personal sacred space that acts as an extra shield against the noise of the outside world. It will also, with respectful practice, create a place outside of time and space in which the Luminous Beings can meet with you, and assist you in your personal healing, your healing work with others or your divination work. It is important to always open this personal sacred space thoughtfully and with intention if you want it to be truly effective. It is also important to close it when you are done with your ceremonies or healings.

The Q'ero or Peruvian Shaman experience the Wiracocha as their soul component and consider themselves connected to Spirit through their ninth chakra. The ninth chakra is shared by everyone. It is the entrance into the space of creation, to the field of all possibility. It is outside of time and space. The eighth and ninth chakras are connected by a luminous cord a Shaman can learn to travel upon to experience the vast expansiveness of creation.

The process of opening the Wiracocha:

1. Bring your hands in front of your heart in a prayer position or pose.
2. Hold the prayer pose for a moment to connect with the Earthkeepers then slowly raise your hands straight up until they are above the head and you sense them entering the globe that is the eighth chakra, usually about 6–12 inches above your head.
3. Turn your palms outward and slowly like a peacock opening its fan extend your arms outward bringing them slowly down until your hands touch your sides, then bring your hands back to the prayer position over your heart.
4. When you have finished the work you are doing, bring your hands back to your sides and slowly lift your arms out and up, like closing a fan, to the top of your head to bring the energy back to the eighth chakra, then lower the hands to the prayer position over your heart.
5. End with your hands in a prayer position for a moment, then lay your palms flat on the heart chakra in a symbol of gratitude, Ayni or reciprocity.

TRANSFORMATIONAL FIRE CEREMONY

The Shamanic tradition of the Munay-Ki is considered a rapid path to enlightenment, a path of Fire or lightning and the Fire ceremony represents this rapid path. It is used to germinate the seeds that you are gifted during the Rites helping them grow, allowing your personal healing to come up gently. Representing the Sun, it is one way we participate in growing the seeds that are planted in the Luminous Energy Field during the Munay-Ki Rites. It is helpful to do a Fire ceremony at least once a week to release that which no longer serves you and to grow and expand that which does, those things the seeds represent.

To create a Fire ceremony find a place that is quiet and calm where you will not be disturbed. It could be next to your Fire place, around some candles, outdoors by a bonfire, or even in an area where you can sit or stand in the sun. Prepare yourself and the space by smudging whenever possible, but do not be dogmatic about that. Often an impromptu ceremony in front of the setting or rising sun can be extremely powerful!

Sit around the Fire or something that represents a Fire, like a group of candles. After preparing the area around you, open sacred space. Then open your personal sacred space over yourself and again over the Fire. Now begin the ceremony by placing your hands on your heart taking a few moments to connect to the Earthkeepers mentally. Next, hold your hands toward the Fire or your symbolic Fire for a moment then bring them to the chakra the seeds of a particular Rite were placed in. State the affirmation that correlates to that Rite and the particular chakra you are working with. Then return your hands to the Fire to repeat the process moving them to the next chakra a seed was placed in.

When you are finished charging all the seeds of a particular Rite you return your hands to the Fire then back to your heart to affirm the process and allow the energy of the Rite to set in before moving on to feed the seeds of the next Rite. When you have had all the Rites and have charged all your seeds, you usually just feed them all at one time during a Fire ceremony. When a group meets to do the Fire ceremony it is appropriate to feed all the seeds of all the Rites at once or just the specific seeds they have received.

Even if you have not had the Munay-Ki Rites, to ask for enlightenment through the chakras by bringing light to them during a Fire ceremony will empower you. You may include additional affirmations after feeding the seeds as well, but it is a choice. Your Fire ceremony can be as short or as long as you choose. Again, do what feels right for you. Remember the Sun is also used as a source of Fire, so sitting in the Sun and opening personal space then feeding your seeds also assists in growing them. Advanced Shaman often use the Sun to feed their seeds, or pull the smoke and Fire energy over them as if they are smudging with the Fire.

Remember to close your personal sacred space taking yourself of the Fire as well. When you are finished, close the larger sacred space. When you finish your ceremony, end with a prayer. Here is an example of an ending prayer I like to use. *"Beauty is before me, Beauty is behind me, Beauty surrounds me, I walk in Beauty."* After the Fire ceremony, it is good to journal your thoughts, or to express them with others that may be joining you in your ceremony. You can use a stone, passing it around to each participant one at a time, and whoever has the stone is the only one allowed to talk. This gives each person the opportunity to be heard unconditionally.

Fire Ceremony for the Nine Rites of the Munay-Ki

The Healer Rite – The seeds this Rite planted can be germinated and grown using conscious intention during the Fire ceremony to activate your personal healing, and your healing gifts.

For the Healer Rite you will want to direct the energy of the Fire first into your hands by reaching toward the Fire, then into the chakras associated with the three aspects of the Healer. These being the work, the heart, and the wisdom of a Healer. For example: reach your hands toward the Fire then bring your hands to your heart to start the ceremony. Now reach toward the Fire, then taking the Fire to the second chakra by placing your hands close to the second chakra say, "I feed the seeds of the work of a healer." Then take your hands back to the Fire then to the heart chakra while saying, "I feed the seeds of the heart of a healer." Again, take your hands to the Fire then bring them to the sixth chakra saying, "I feed the seeds of the wisdom of a healer." You would then reach for the Fire, then bring your hands to your heart. An additional affirmation that could be stated at this point of the ceremony follows.

Healer Rite Affirmation – *I am now connected to a lineage of Earthkeepers that come and assist me with my personal healing in a gentle way on an energetic level. They assist in healing the wound from my ancestors. I am now able to heal myself and others.*

The Bands of Power Rite – The seeds this Rite planted can be germinated and grown using conscious intention during the Fire ceremony to activate the five bands of power that will protect you and allow you to walk in the world with grace.

First direct the energy of the Fire into your hands by reaching toward the Fire then bring your hands to your heart to start the ceremony. Now reach toward the Fire directing the energy into your hands, then taking the Fire to the navel chakra by placing your hands on or close to the second chakra say, "I feed the seeds of the first band of power, Earth." Then take your hands back to the Fire, then to the solar plexus chakra saying, "I feed the seeds of the second

156

band of power, Water." Again take your hands to the Fire then bring them to the heart chakra saying, "I feed the seeds of the third band of power, Fire." Now reach toward the Fire, then taking the Fire to the throat chakra by placing your hands on or close to that chakra saying, "I feed the seeds of the fourth band of power, Air." Then take your hands back to the Fire then to the forehead or third eye chakra saying, "I feed the seeds of the fifth band of power, Spirit." Again take your hands to the Fire then bring them to the crown chakra or top of your head, then pull up and out drawing a rainbow light out the top of the head and down the body connecting all the bands of power together. Do this twice. Reach for the Fire then bring the hands to your heart to end the ceremony. An additional affirmation that could be stated at this point of the ceremony follows.

Bands of Power Rite Affirmation - *Five energetic bands of power surround me and protect me breaking down any negative energy that comes my way. I now walk in safety and grace in the world.*

The first band of power is Earth, it is black, and covers the support and navel chakras. The second band of power is Water. It is red and covers the solar plexus chakra. The third band of power is Fire. It is gold and covers the heart chakra. The fourth band of power is Air. It is Silver and covers the throat chakra. The fifth band of power is Spirit. It is white and covers the third eye chakra. The rainbow fountain is pulled out of the crown chakra.

The Harmony Rite - The seeds this Rite planted can be germinated and grown using conscious intention during the Fire ceremony to activate the energies and protection of the archetypes.

First direct the energy of the Fire into your hands by reaching toward the Fire then bring your hands to your heart to start the ceremony. Now reach toward the Fire directing the energy into your hands, then taking the Fire to the first chakra by placing your hands close to the first chakra say, "I feed the seeds of the Serpent to help me shed my past." Then take your hands back to the Fire then toward the second chakra while saying, "I feed the seeds of the Jaguar, to help me become a warrior without enemies." Again take

157

your hands to the Fire then bring them to the third chakra while saying, "I feed the seeds of the Hummingbird, to help me make the journey to wholeness." Now reach toward the Fire, then take the Fire to the fourth chakra by placing your hands close to that chakra while saying, "I feed the seeds of the Eagle and Condor, to help me see from a higher perspective." Next, take your hands back to the Fire then to the fifth chakra saying, "I feed the seeds of Huascar, who balances my shadow." Again take your hands to the Fire then bring them to the sixth chakra saying, "I feed the seeds of the Quetzalcoatl, who helps me balance the middle world, my conscious mind." Now reach toward the Fire, then taking the Fire to the crown chakra by placing your hands on or close to that chakra saying, "I feed the seeds of Pachakuti, who brings me into circular time and all possibilities." Take your hands back to the Fire then to the heart chakra. An additional affirmation that could be stated at this point of the ceremony follows.

Harmony Rite Affirmation – *The seven archetypes are now within my chakras. They now assist me in bringing up, transmuting and burning up all that no longer serves me. The Serpent sheds my past. Jaguar helps me step beyond fear. Hummingbird helps me undertake and accomplish my journey. Eagle sees with the eyes of the heart, from a higher perspective. Huascar, harmonizes my relationship with my shadow. Quetzalcoatl organizes my relationship with the middle world. Pachakuti embodies circular time and brings me into all possibilities.*

The Seer Rite – The seeds this Rite planted can be germinated and grown using conscious intention during the Fire ceremony to activate the crown and the necklace of light.

First, direct the energy of the Fire into your hands by reaching toward the Fire then bring your hands to your heart to start the ceremony. Next, reach toward the Fire directing the energy into your hands then take them to the top of your head while visualizing the Crown of Light on your head. Take your hands back to the Fire then place one hand at the third eye and one at the back of your head at the area of the visual cortex and say, "I feed the seeds of the crown of light." Now reach toward the Fire directing the energy into your hands, then take one hand to the heart chakra and place the other at the back of your head at the area of the visual cortex. While visualizing the necklace, say, "I feed the seeds of the Necklace of Light." Next, reach for the Fire then bring the hands to your third eye. Reach toward the Fire again, then to your heart to end the ceremony. An additional affirmation that could be stated at this point of the ceremony follows.

Seer Rite Affirmation – *I now have a Crown of Light and Necklace of Light which awaken my ability to perceive the invisible world. I now see aspects of myself and others I have not previously seen. I am willing to perceive everything.*

The Daykeeper Rite – The seeds this Rite planted can be germinated and grown using conscious intention during the Fire ceremony to activate the connection to the lineage of the Daykeepers, the past masters that tended ancient altars.

First, direct the energy of the Fire into your hands by reaching toward the Fire then bring your hands to your heart to start the ceremony. Next, reach toward the Fire then place your hands close to the second chakra and say, "I feed the seeds of the work of a Daykeeper." Then take your hands back to the Fire then to the heart chakra while saying, "I feed the seeds of the heart of a Daykeeper." Again take your hands to the Fire then bring them to the sixth chakra saying, "I feed the seeds of the wisdom and vision of a Daykeeper." Reach for the Fire then bring your hands to your crown chakra, feeding the seeds of the Daykeeper lineage saying, "I feed the seeds of the lineage of the Daykeepers." Reach toward the Fire again, then to your heart to end the ceremony. An additional affirmation that could be stated at this point of the ceremony follows.

Daykeeper Rite Affirmation – *I am connected to the lineage of the Daykeepers, past Masters that tended sacred altars. I am now able to call upon those ancient altars to help heal and bring balance to myself and to the Earth. I am healing my inner feminine, stepping beyond fear and practicing peace. I have recovered that part of me that always walks in beauty.*

159

The Wisdomkeeper Rite – The seeds this Rite planted can be germinated and grown using conscious intention during the Fire ceremony to activate the connection to the lineage of the Wisdomkeepers that protect the ancient teaching.

First, direct the energy of the Fire into your hands by reaching toward the Fire then bring your hands to your heart to start the ceremony. Next, reach toward the Fire then place your hands close to the second chakra and say, "I feed the seeds of the work of a Wisdomkeeper." Take your hands back to the Fire then to the heart chakra while saying, "I feed the seeds of the heart of a Wisdomkeeper." Again take your hands to the Fire then bring them to the sixth chakra while saying, "I feed the seeds of the wisdom and vision of a Wisdomkeeper." Reach for the Fire then bring your hands to your crown chakra, feeding the seeds of the Wisdomkeeper lineage saying, "I feed the seeds of the lineage of the Wisdomkeepers." Reach toward the Fire again, then to your heart to end the ceremony. An additional affirmation that could be stated at this point of the ceremony follows.

Wisdomkeeper Rite Affirmation – *I am connected to the lineage of the Wisdomkeepers, medicine men and women that protect the ancient medicine teachings and share them with others when appropriate. I am connected to the spirits of the mountains. I am now able to step out of time and taste infinity. I am healing the wounds from my past lives and my inner masculine.*

The Earthkeeper Rite – The seeds this Rite planted can be germinated and grown using conscious intention during the Fire ceremony to activate the connection to the Luminous Beings that are the guardians of our galaxy, and the stewards of all life on Earth. They can be summoned to bring healing and balance to any situation.

First, direct the energy of the Fire into your hands by reaching toward the Fire then bring your hands to your heart to start the ceremony. Next, reach toward the Fire then place your hands close to the second chakra and say, "I feed the seeds of the work of an Earthkeeper." Take your hands back to the Fire then to the heart

chakra while saying, "I feed the seeds of the heart of an Earthkeeper."
Again take your hands to the Fire then bring them to the sixth
chakra while saying, "I feed the seeds of the wisdom and vision of
an Earthkeeper." Reach for the Fire then bring your hands to your
crown chakra, feeding the seeds of the Earthkeeper lineage saying,
"I feed the seeds of the lineage of the Earthkeepers." Reach toward
the Fire again, then to your heart to end the ceremony. An additional
affirmation that could be stated at this point of the ceremony follows.

Earthkeeper Rite Affirmation – *I am connected to the Luminous
Beings that are the guardians of our galaxy. I am protected by these guardians,
the stewards of all life on Earth, and can summon their power to bring healing
and balance to any situation.*

The Starkeeper Rite – The seeds this Rite planted can be
germinated and grown using conscious intention during the Fire
ceremony to activate the connection to the Starkeepers who anchor
us safely in life, both in the future and to life now in this time of
great change. They help us evolve into Homo Luminous light beings.

First, direct the energy of the Fire into your hands by reaching
toward the Fire then bring your hands to your heart to start the
ceremony. Next, reach toward the Fire then place your hands close to
the first chakra by placing your hands close to the first chakra, then
return to the Fire. Continue this pattern quietly without affirmations
for each of the seven chakras. As you feed the seeds in each chakra, in
quiet, recall these seeds have the codes for the new body, that of Homo
Luminous. Be thankful that the Christ or Buddha Consciousness has
begun to awaken in you and that you have now become a 'Child of
the Sun' who is connected to the stars. When you have finished with
each chakra, take your hands back to the Fire then bring them back
to the heart chakra. An additional affirmation that could be stated at
this point of the ceremony follows.

Starkeeper Rite Affirmation – *I am now anchored safely to the
future, to the time after the great change. I have acquired stewardship of the
time to come. I am evolving into a Homo Luminous light being. I am now
resistant to disease and my ageing process has slowed down.*

The Creator Rite – The seeds this Rite planted can be germinated and grown using conscious intention during the Fire ceremony to activate the connection of the Creators and awaken your ability to dream creation into being.

First, direct the energy of the Fire into your hands by reaching toward the Fire then bring your hands to your heart to start the ceremony. Next, reach toward the Fire then place your hands close to the second chakra and say, "I am the work of a Creator." Take your hands back to the Fire then to the heart chakra while saying, "I am the heart of a Creator." Again take your hands to the Fire then bring them to the sixth chakra while saying, "I am the wisdom and vision of a Creator." Reach for the Fire then bring your hands to your crown chakra, feeding the seeds of the Creators saying, "I am connected to the lineage of the Creators." Now reach toward the Fire, arms spread open slightly, hands open, and palms facing the fire saying, "I feed the seeds of the Munay-Ki." Stay in this space quietly for a while, allowing the Fire to germinate all your seeds. When you are ready, reach for the Fire then bring your hands to your heart. An affirmation that could be stated at this point of this ceremony follows.

Creator Rite Affirmation – *I am now an access point to the matrix of creation. My energy field is unbound from time and I now dream the world into being. I am a conduit between the manifested and un-manifested world.*

After the ceremony, remember to close your personal sacred space, then the larger sacred space, ending with a prayer: *"Beauty is before me, Beauty is behind me, Beauty surrounds me, I walk in Beauty."* More prayers may be given at any time.

After the ceremony, it is a good idea to record your experience in a journal. If you are working with a group, this is a good time to allow each person to speak or share. You can use a stone, passing it around to each participant one at a time, and whoever has the stone is the only one allowed to talk. This gives each person the opportunity to be heard unconditionally.

Until you have received all the Rites of the Munay-Ki, only perform the sections of the Fire ceremony with the Rites you have received. You can still do a Fire ceremony if you are with people who have not had any of the Munay-Ki rites during other ceremonies you attend because anytime you bring Fire and light to the chakras you are increasing self-empowerment. However, with others that have not had the Rites, I would do the Fire ceremony in a way similar to feeding the seeds of the Starkeeper Rite, bringing light to all the chakras but in silence. You may add prayers, but they should not affirm the Rites or the seeds because the participants have no seeds to germinate. You would still prepare the space and the participants with smudge before the ceremony and open the large sacred space, but not necessarily the personal sacred space. I would also begin and end the ceremony with prayer.

After you have received all the Rites of the Munay-Ki, you can do the Fire ceremony going through all the seeds feeding sections for more empowerment, or just sit in the presence of the Fire or Sun opening yourself to the energy, reaching toward the Fire opening your hands in an open receiving Mudra, (hands open, palms toward the Fire) and saying, "I feed the seeds of the Munay-Ki." Stay in this space quietly for a while, allowing the Fire to germinate all your seeds at once. Again, I would still open sacred space, personal sacred space, and begin and end with prayer.

Munay-Ki Affirmations

May be used with Fire Ceremony, or
anytime as a blessing or invocation.

HEALER – I am now connected to a lineage of Earthkeepers that come and assist me with my personal healing in a gentle way on an energetic level. They assist in healing the wound from my ancestors. I am now able to heal myself and others.

BANDS OF POWER – Five energetic bands of power surround me and protect me breaking down any negative energy that comes my way. I now walk in safety and grace in the world.

HARMONY – The seven archetypes are now within my chakras. They now assist me in bringing up, transmuting and burning up all that no longer serves me. The Serpent sheds my past. Jaguar helps me step beyond fear. Hummingbird helps me undertake and accomplish my journey. Eagle sees with the eyes of the heart, from a higher perspective. Huascar, harmonizes my relationship with my shadow. Quetzalcoatl organizes my relationship with the middle world. Pachakuti embodies circular time and brings me into all possibilities.

SEER – I now have a Crown of Light and Necklace of Light which awaken my ability to perceive the invisible world. I now see aspects of myself and others I have not previously seen. I am willing to perceive everything.

DAYKEEPERS – I am connected to the lineage of the Daykeepers, past Masters that tended sacred altars. I am now able to call upon those ancient altars to help heal and bring balance to myself and to the Earth. I am healing my inner feminine, stepping beyond fear and practicing peace. I have recovered that part of me that always walks in beauty.

WISDOMKEEPERS – I am connected to the lineage of the Wisdomkeepers, medicine men and women that protect the ancient medicine teachings and share them with others when appropriate. I am connected to the spirits of the mountains. I am now able to step out of time and taste infinity. I am healing the wounds from my past lives and my inner masculine.

EARTHKEEPERS – I am connected to the Luminous Beings that are the guardians of our galaxy. I am protected by these guardians, the stewards of all life on Earth, and can summon their power to bring healing and balance to any situation.

STARKEEPERS – I am now anchored safely to the future and the time after the great change. I have acquired stewardship of the time to come. I have acquired stewardship of the time to come. I am evolving into a Homo Luminous light being. I am now resistant to disease and my ageing process has slowed down.

CREATORS – I am now an access point to the matrix of creation. My energy field is unbound from time and I now dream the world into being. I am a conduit between the manifested and un-manifested world.

PRAYER – Thank you Divine Source for bringing me closer to a deeper connection to You, for opening me to my well-being and manifesting beauty, joy, and prosperity in my life. I open to your guidance and move toward my good. Beauty is before me, Beauty is behind me, Beauty surrounds me, I walk in Beauty.

THE PRINCIPLES OF THE BEAUTY WAY

The Munay-Ki, the Energy of Love

T he Beauty Way teaches that the Shaman is to be alert at all times to synchronicity, to listen to messages from nature striving to create harmony between thoughts, things, and events. They are to acknowledge the wholeness of being that is the Earth and to sense the interconnectedness of the visible and invisible Universe. The Shaman's path is the way of light. They work to over-come their own self-limiting ideas and to be free of the opinions of others. The five principles of the Munay-Ki give a basis to accomplish these goals.

Similar to most spiritual traditions, there are ethical principles in the teachings of the Beauty Way. These principles demonstrate the Earth based world view of the Q'ero, or Andean Peruvian Shaman. They include: Munay, practice loving kindness and live life in beauty; Yachay, develop correct knowledge guided by wisdom; Llank'ay, live with right action, do good work and leave a legacy; Kawsay, respect life and all life-sustaining processes, know that there is energy in all things; and Ayni, give back in appreciation, circulate your energy, goods, and knowledge for the benefit of the whole.

Munay (moon-eye) – to practice loving kindness and live your life in beauty

Munay means to love, a deep abiding, impersonal love that comes naturally from the heart. This love does not expect anything in return, but simply radiates emotional warmth and caring. It is a love of acceptance. When one loves in this manner, thoughtfulness and kindness follow. It is loving kindness. It not only means a nourishing, all-encompassing love, but also signifies tranquility and beauty, suggesting pleasant experiences and tranquility within and without. Beauty is the outer wrapping, kindness with love the inside. In this tradition, beauty and love are inseparable. When you have these in your heart you are peaceful. Munay is inherent in nature, a stunning sunset or a luscious fruit, and it is a quality inside of us as well. When both the outer and inner world reflects love and beauty, one manifests benevolence in action and character. To experience Munay, we must cultivate it through conscious acts of kindness. To share the beauty of nature is one way to share Munay or love with others.

Yachay (yach-eye) – developing correct knowledge guided by wisdom

This second principle is based on the lifestyle of the Q'ero, the indigenous Peruvian people that protected and passed on the original Shamanic lineage of the Munay-Ki. They had to remember and learn from the experiences of their ancestors to master the lifestyle which required them to live above 14,000 feet in the mountains. They knew it was their responsibility to pass on what they had learned to future generations for their survival as well. This included knowledge of information on healing plants, how to cultivate the soil, care for animals, and other skills for survival as well as spiritual truths. So Yachay is essential knowledge shared with others which determines survival and the continuation of a way of life physically as well as spiritually. Yachay also means to be flexible in thought and action and to know that true knowledge comes from direct personal experience guided by insight and intuition. Yachay includes letting go of opinions, judgmental behavior, and the idea that accumulation of information produces knowledge. Knowledge is acquired through carefully sifting through the facts and rearranging information to form a mental map that is true and useful for us. Too much information, even if supported by facts, often leads to confusion or dogma. Yachay also implies unlearning and knowing that true knowledge does not have to be defended.

Llank'ay (lonk-eye) - right action, to do good work and leave a legacy

This third principle's literal translation is 'to work'. But it goes beyond physical labor to include mental and creative work, as well as performing ceremonies and healing. Ceremonial life imbues work with meaning. It is not isolated from physical work. Balancing outer activity with inner work is the key to survival.

Though each of the first three principles seems separate with their own characteristics, they work together. Munay or love and beauty make daily life pleasing softening the hard edges of difficulty. Without initiating right action or Llank'ay, nothing gets done, things stagnate. Yet, action for its own sake can lead to conflict. The best outcome of action proceeds from knowledge, Yachay, the second principle. Each principle transforms into a higher form as we learn and grow. Munay becomes impersonal love that embraces all things. Yachay becomes the superior consciousness one arrives at through the proper cultivation of love through work. And Llank'ay which starts as just work and routine ritual becomes right livelihood. It is a way of living that is ecologically sound, promotes the welfare of others, and encourages service performed in the Spirit of loving kindness. Another way to look at these principles is that they consist of the ability to feel, think, and act. When they are in harmony, they balance the individual.

Kawsay (cows-eye) – respect for life and all life-sustaining processes

Kawsay means life, and refers to the respect of the matrix of energy or the web of life that links all living things on Earth. To the Andean, and most indigenous cultures, Pachamama or Mother Earth, is not just the ground we live on that supports all things, but it is imbued with life-giving energy. Through this energy all life is connected. This intertwining of life and energy is Kawsay Pacha, the world of living energy.

All natural things are material yet possess an innate intelligence. Mountains or Apus (ah-poos) are respected as natural temples and as powerful Spiritual Beings that communicate and influence the destiny of man. Lightning, thunder, animals, trees, rocks, birds, insects, mountains, lakes, rivers, rainbows, earthquakes, hail, snow, ice and rain all have a luminous counterpart that can communicate with humans in an intuitive way. To live a harmonious life, it is necessary to balance the human sphere and the environmental forces. Respecting the life force or energy within all things, and all life-sustaining processes, gives us access to this life force or energy. Truly understanding this connection between the life force within all things, gives us the ability to transmute energy. This understanding moves us to respect and protect all life on the planet, to protect the trees, the water, the animals, the air, and all aspects of Mother Earth! We come to understand that all life is sacred and is deserving of respect!

Ceremonies play a significant role in maintaining respect, an attunement or connection with the world of living energy. The way we live is as important as how we ceremonially interact with the forces of life. Balance between daily life and ritual is maintained through the practice of reciprocity or Ayni (eye-knee).

Ayni (eye-knee) – to give back, circulate energy, goods, knowledge and labor for the benefit of family, society and culture out of respect and the understanding of reciprocity

This principle is the single most important concept of the Shamanic Andean way. It includes respect for all things and reciprocity. It allows all five principles to work synergistically and complete the circle of life. It is the interchange of energy through works, deeds, actions, thoughts, and emotions, between individuals and the Universe. It provides purpose for all the other principles and makes them function.

Ayni is living life through acts of reciprocity. Reciprocity is the interchange of loving kindness, knowledge, and the fruits of one's labor between humans and nature Spirits. It is giving to receive, and receiving so we can give. It implies that one's labor is shared. The trees give us oxygen and we give them carbon dioxide, it is a mutual exchange.

It also implies respect for others, their work, thoughts, feelings, and knowledge. Respect is the key to understanding the Andean, and many indigenous cultural ways. When we return the good that comes to us showing respect, without judging the giver or what is received, it becomes benevolence in its highest form.

Ayni is deeper than mutual respect and helping others, it implies the conscious, willing acknowledgement of the interconnection between humans and the natural world that sustains them. To the Andean Shaman, the Earth is shared by all things visible and invisible. The energetic interchange between the two is the work of the Shaman or priest. The Ceremonies that are performed are symbolic acts of reciprocity. Respect and reciprocity are not exclusive to Ceremonies but are to be included in everyday life.

Brief Definition of Terms

Apukuna – Mountain Spirits or the male aspect of the Divine

Ayni (eye-knee) – To give back, circulate energy, goods, knowledge and labor for the benefit of society

Chakana – Three stepped symmetric cross with a hole in the center of it. It represents the Southern Cross constellation believed by the ancient Andeans to be the center of the Universe.

Chaskakuna – The Stars

Despacho – The give-away ceremony of Ayni, used to shift, balance, and manifest in our lives.

Huáscar (circa 1502-1532) – The keeper of the lower world who brings harmony and peace to our subconscious mind. He resides in the throat chakra.

Hucha (who-cha) – Disorganized energy

Hucha Mikhuy (Mee-kwee) – Advanced technique to clear hucha.

Inti – The Sun

Journey – An active meditation, usually done while listening to a drum or rattle allowing you to travel to the other realms assisting you in accessing Divine Revelation.

Kallpa – An innate intelligence in all things.

Kawsay (cows-eye) – Universe or Cosmos, a respect for life, and life-sustaining processes

Kawak – References to a 'seer' or individual who can perceive projections

Laika – Medicine people and Earthkeepers of the Q'ero. Connected to the original Shamanic lineage, they protected the processes of the Munay-Ki.

Llank'ay (lonk-eye) – Right action, good work, to leave a legacy.

Mandala – A graphic cosmic symbol used as a meditation aid

Mesa – traveling altar, or personal medicine bundle of power objects

Munay-Ki Rites – Ceremonial Rites that connect you to the energy of the Earth Keepers, Shaman that have come before us and those that will come after us that protect and honor the planet.

Munay (moon-eye) – To practice loving kindness and live your life in beauty and love.

Pachakuti – The great Inka king that represents the aspects that connect us to the time to come, to who we are becoming and allows us to step into circular time connecting to all possibilities. He resides in the crown chakra.

Pachamama – The Earth or the Great Mother, the Goddess

Paqos (pah-ko) – Shaman

Pi Stone – Round stone with a hole in the center that represents the Luminous Energy Field

Power animals – Spirit animals that assist and travel with us during this earthly life. They lend us their energy for our assistance, and guide a Shaman during journey.

Poq'po (pok-po) – The human energy body

Q'ero –The indigenous Peruvian people who speak Quechua.

Qosqo (Kos-ko) – The Spiritual stomach, an entrance into the Spiritual bodies.

Quetzalcoatl – The keeper of the middle physical world who brings harmony and order to our present lives, resides in the third eye.

Saminchukuy (sah-min-chas-ka) – Technique to clear and release disorganized energy

Sami (sahm-ee) – Ordered energy, our natural state

Wiracocha – Peruvian God of Creation, term for the eighth or Soul Star chakra above your head.

Yachay (yach-eye) – Developing correct knowledge guided by wisdom

ABOUT THE AUTHORS

Michael and Laura have been working and teaching with various energy healing modalities since the early 1990's. Reiki Master Teachers and Shamanic practitioners, they are Natural Health Facilitators, intuitive consultants, energy workers/healers, readers and teachers. They practice Nature Spirituality and profess the Unity principles. Along with their classes in yoga, T'ai Chi, meditation, and Reiki, they teach Ceremonial Shamanism while sharing the Munay-Ki Rites.

After completing the nine Munay-Ki Rites of the Peruvian Mountain Shaman they felt called to Machu Picchu, Peru where their pilgrimage led them both to be initiated by the Guardian Spirit of the area. This experience was so life changing and profound that when they returned, their main focus became sharing the teachings of the Beauty Way, Ceremonial Shamanism. This book is compiled from their lectures, to be used by readers for self-empowerment, and for teachers of the Munay-Ki Rites.

Laura is degreed with a Masters in Holistic Nutrition, a Bachelors of General Studies from Texas Christian University, and in Professional Interior Design through the Sheffield School of Interior Design. They are both certified as Sei Chem and Tibetan Reiki Master Teachers and in T'ai Chi, Yoga, and Hwal Ki Do Korean Acupressure.

Along with their classes, they provide private healing sessions using Hwal Ki Do, Reiki, Crystals, Feng Shui, Shamanic Soul Retrieval, Numerology, Animal Cards, Runes, Andean Sol Rocks, and lifestyle/nutritional counseling. Contact the authors at WalkingtheBeautyWay.com or Ftha-ul.com

May You Always Walk in Beauty
Into the Golden Age of Dreaming!